Basic Busines:
The 700 Comn

Pitman 2000 Shorthand

Edith Searle

PITMAN PUBLISHING
128 Long Acre, London WC2E 9AN
A Division of Longman Group UK Limited

© Sir Isaac Pitman Limited 1991

First published in Great Britain 1991

British Library Cataloguing in Publication Data
Searle, Edith
    Basic business dictation.
    1. Pitman Shorthand. Dictation
    I. Title
    653.424042

    ISBN 0–273–03419–7

Typeset by ⊼ Tek Art Ltd, Addiscombe, Croydon, Surrey
Printed and bound in Great Britain.

Pitman ▦

Contents

Introduction

The aim of this book is to ensure that students know the shorthand outlines for the 700 most common words in the English language and can read and write them without hesitation. These words, together with their derivatives, form approximately 80 per cent of all general written material.

The book is divided into 12 sections, each on a different theme, so that the material can be covered at evening classes in one term, or in a correspondingly shorter period in full-time education. It has the following main applications:

Theory consolidation

To provide a link in the learning process between completion of the theory and concentrated dictation and speed development. Students can either learn the words in each section, in preparation for the dictation, or the passages may be dictated first and then checked. Any necessary remedial work should then be carried out before the dictation is repeated.

Speed development

To provide dictation which students should be able to take at a speed higher than for dictation based on a more general vocabulary. Rapid reading of the shorthand passages will help in speed development.

Individual progress

The cassettes will enable students who use this book to progress at their own individual speed. This will be particularly useful for those planning to return to work who wish to improve their speeds.

Word lists

Each section is preceded by a word list, divided into three parts, introducing the new words used in the relevant passages which follow. Under the heading of *derivatives* are words derived from the root word in that particular section or a previous section. A few *additional* words have been introduced into each section, which may either be given to students before dictation or used as a challenge.

Each section contains dictation passages of 100, 150 and 180 words, marked in tens for dictation at any desired speed. In this way the book gives ample scope for the learning of these common words in easy stages, giving students confidence in reading and writing them.

This is an essential book for both the teacher and the student, who should make use of the word lists and read the shorthand at the end of the book.

The book presents a new approach to dictation, the passages covering only the words given for the particular or preceding sections. The words and passages are built up progressively, using a limited number of new words in each section.

I should like to thank Bryan Coombs for reading the manuscript and giving his help and advice in the preparation of this book.

Edith Searle

New short forms

advantage		impossible	
advertise/ advertisement		inconvenience/ inconvenient/ inconveniently	
advertised		indifferent	
advertising		insurance	
behalf		maximum	
character		minimum	
characteristic		misrepresent	
different/difference		November	
differently		number	
disadvantage		opinion	
during		opportunity	
everything		principle/principal/ principally	
February		represent	
financial/financially		representation	
general/generally		representative	
however		significance	
importance/important		signify/significant	
importantly			

vi

sure		**New intersection**
unusual/unusually		
usual/usually		morning

CHAPTER 1
The business show

This section consists of an advertisement for a Business Show to be held in Southsea (100 words); a circular letter to stand holders at the show, giving details for setting up the show and clearing the site afterwards (150 words); and a memo to the Head of the Advertising Department about advertisements and free tickets (180 words).

1A   Word list

a/an	day	inform-ation		
all	deliver	is/his		
and	early	it		
any/in	every	kind		
are	for	large		
at	from	machine		
business	further	man		
buy/by	ground	may		
car	high	most		
come	his/is	Mrs		
country	hope	must		
date	in/any			

2

near		station	representatives
next		take	
of		the	stationery
on		there/their	taken
one		thing	welcome
order		to	
organise		up	**Additional words**
own		way/weigh	admission
party		well	firm
place		will	park
point		world	
pound		write/right	**Phrases/intersection**
rail			further information
represent		**Derivatives**	in the business
right/write		delivery	in the country
see/sea		largest	take place
show		machinery	up-to-date
south		organiser	
stand			

1B Word list

advertise/–ment

after

be

before

best

can

clear

copy

dear

expert

free

good

help

hold

I/eye

if

insurance

issue

make

or

out

please

product

responsible/responsibility

set

sir

success

sure

that

time

together

too/two

we

when

who

wish

with

you

your

Derivatives

cannot

holder

successful

Additional words

accept

arrive

enclose

faithfully

madam

site/sight

ten

ticket

twenty

4

Phrases		

at all times		Dear Sir or Madam		will you please	
in any way		your own			
best wishes		it will be		yours faithfully	

1C Word list

agree		head		so/sew/sow	
am		idea		soon	
as/has		let		thank	
ask		letter		them	
attention		like		they	
black		line		think	
charge		me		thousand	
colour		Mr		through	
different/difference		my		trade/toward	
each		paper		under	
ease		possible		very	
has/as		sale/sail		word	
have		sent		would	
he		should			

writing .... local .... as soon as we can ....

print ....

Derivative

easier ....

Additional words

depart-ment ....

draw ....

Phrases/intersections

advertis-ing de-partment ....

as soon as possible ....

if you will ....

in charge of ....

sales de-partment ....

thank you ....

they are ....

two thousand ....

1A The business show

An advertisement for The Southsea Business Show.

THE SOUTHSEA BUSINESS SHOW
will take place
at
The Show[10] Ground
High Point
SOUTHSEA
from 16 to 20 May

The[20] largest show of its kind in the country – a 'must'[30] for everyone in the business world.

Everything on show, from[40] stationery to the most up-to-date machinery.

All stands[50] are manned by the firms' own representatives. Orders taken for[60] early delivery.

The Show Ground is next to the railway[70] station, and there is a car park nearby.

Admission for[80] the day £1. Parties welcome.

For further information write[90] to:
Mrs Hope
Organiser
Business Show
at the Show Ground[100]

(*The shorthand for this passage is printed on page 71.*)

1B   The business show

A circular letter to all stand holders at the Show.

To all Stand Holders

Dear Sir or Madam

THE SOUTHSEA[10] BUSINESS SHOW
16 to 20 May

I enclose 10 copies[20] of the advertisement for the Business Show, together with 20[30] tickets for free admission.

The Show Ground will be free[40] for 2 days before the Show, when you may set[50] up your stand, and for one day after the Show[60] to clear the site.

Will you please make sure that[70] your stand is manned at all times by one of[80] your own representatives who is an expert on your products[90] and can take orders.

It will be your responsibility to[100] take out your own insurance; we cannot accept responsibility for[110] your goods.

Stand holders' car parking tickets are enclosed. Tickets[120] for your representatives will be issued at the ground when[130] you arrive.

Please write if I can help in any[140] way.

With best wishes for a successful Show,

Yours faithfully[150]
(*The shorthand for this passage is printed on page 72.*)

1C The business show

Memo to the Head of the Advertising Department about the printing of advertisements and tickets for the Show.

FROM   H Hope

TO   Head of Advertising Department

THE SOUTHSEA[10] BUSINESS SHOW

Thank you for letting me see the Show[20] advertisement so soon. It is very good. Will you please[30] have 2000 copies printed as soon as possible. I[40] should like the words 'The Southsea Business Show' to be[50] underlined.

We must place the advertisement in trade and local[60] papers throughout the country as soon as we can. Each[70] firm having a stand in the Show should be sent[80] 10 copies of the advertisement together with 20 tickets for[90] free admission to the Show. I am writing a letter[100] to all stand holders. If you will let me have[110] the advertisements and free tickets when they are printed, I[120] will enclose them with my letters.

I think it would[130] be a good idea to have the free tickets printed[140] in a different colour to make it easier to draw[150] attention to free ticket-holders on admission. Before tickets are[160] printed, please ask Mr Black, Head of Sales Department, if[170] he agrees, as he will be in charge of admissions.[180]

(The shorthand for this passage is printed on pages 72-3.)

CHAPTER 2
Meeting of representatives

This section is about a meeting of representatives of a firm selling cleaning materials, the first passage (100 words) being a memo to the Head of the Personnel Department asking him to arrange the meeting. The second passage (150 words) is a memo to the representatives asking for details of sales and changes in distribution for consideration at the meeting, and the third passage (180 words) is a report of the meeting of the representatives.

2A   Word list

Word	Outline	Word	Outline
April		meet/meat	
board		necessary	
book		no/know	
call		number	
do		person	
great		room	
hear/here		serve	
hour/our		this	
hundred		usual	
mark		Wednes-day	
meal		winter	

Derivatives

Word	Outline
been	
done	
grateful	
personnel	

Additional words

Word	Outline
arrange	
arrange-ments	

10

Intersection

necessary
arrange-
ments

2B Word list

able		matter		greatly	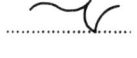
change		month		held	
consider		new/knew		monthly	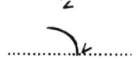
detail		particular			

Additional words

difficult	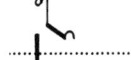	present			
distribute		receive		appreciate	
division		send		area	
during		then	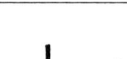		

Phrases

figure		which			
future				I hope	
influence	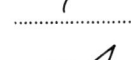			in this matter	

Derivatives

last		distribu-tion
March		to consider
		three months

2C Word list

add		pass		felt	
also		put		given	
better		report			
clean		these		**Additional words**	
end		town		concern	
feel		train		range	
form		was		scent	
give		were		transport	
had		where			
low		while		**Phrase**	
not				had not been	
note		**Derivatives**			
other		consider-ation			

12

2A Meeting of representatives

Memo asking the Head of Personnel Department to make
arrangements for a meeting of all representatives.

TO   Head of Personnel Department

FROM   Mark Winter, Sales Department[10]

As it is time to call the next meeting of [20] representatives, I should be
grateful if you would make the[30] necessary arrangements for me. I
should like to hold it[40] on Wednesday, 30 April, at 1000 hours in the[50]
Board Room. Will you please book the room and arrange[60] for the usual
kind of meal to be served at[70] 1300 hours. As soon as I hear from you[80]
that this has been done, I will write to the[90] representatives, and let you
know numbers when I have them.[100]

(The shorthand for this passage is printed on pages 73-4.)

2B Meeting of representatives

Memo to all sales representatives asking them to attend a meeting.

TO   All Representatives

FROM   Head of Sales Department

The next[10] three-monthly meeting will be held at 1130 hours[20] on Wednesday, 30 April, in the Board Room, when I[30] hope all representatives will be present. As usual, a meal[40] will be served at 1300 hours.

I should be[50] grateful if you would let me have, as soon as[60] possible, up-to-date figures for sales during the last[70] three months to March, together with any marked changes in[80] the distribution of sales in your particular division. If the[90] figures are received in time, I should like to send[100] details to each of you so that you may have[110] time to consider them before the meeting. We may then[120] be able to come up with new ideas which may[130] influence future sales in difficult areas. Your help in this[140] matter would be greatly appreciated.

Copies to Heads of Departments.[150]

(The shorthand for this passage is printed on pages 74-5.)

14

2C Meeting of representatives

Report of meeting of sales representatives to consider sales of cleaning products.

Report of the meeting of representatives
30 April

All the[10] representatives were present at the meeting, together with the Heads[20] of Sales and Personnel Departments.

The sales figures for the[30] past 3 months were considered in detail. As agreed at[40] the last meeting, scent had been added to our cleaning[50] product range, and it was noted that, in areas where[60] scented products were distributed, sales had been better, while sales[70] in other areas had not been so successful. It was[80] felt that in future all our cleaning products should be[90] scented.

It was also felt that there should be better[100] advertising in these areas of low sales, and that advertisements[110] should be placed in local papers and put up in[120] each town in the areas concerned. It was also agreed[130] that the time taken from the placing of the order[140] to the delivery of goods was too great. Representatives considered[150] that delivery by train had not been successful and that[160] consideration should be given to other forms of transport before[170] the next meeting.

The meeting ended at 1500 hours.[180]

(The shorthand for this passage is printed on page 75.)

CHAPTER 3
The Modern Art Company

The first passage is a circular letter from a firm selling stationery supplies, outlining their plans for expanding their business (100 words). This is followed by a letter of enquiry to the firm from The Modern Art Company about the supply and printing of headed paper (150 words), and the final passage (180 words) is a memo to the Chief Printer asking him to provide information and samples to be sent in reply to the previous letter.

3A   Word list

company	service	expand
course	shall	fifty
depend	year	
distance		**Phrases/intersection**
industry	**Derivatives**	has been
interest	always	in our
mile	produce	our Company
need	receipt	range of the
offer	require-ment	we shall be
plan		we would like
quality	**Additional words**	
require	discuss	

3B Word list

amount	white	deal
art	work	realise
blue		sample
character	**Derivatives**	type
cost	largely	wonder
either	lower	
gold	materials	**Phrases**
important /ce	particu- larly	able to
question		I would like
supply	**Additional words**	it would be
use	accept- able	thank you for your letter
whether		

3C Word list

both	many	summer
chief	modern	
custom	observa- tion	**Derivatives**
leave	self	consider- able
made		

known	......?......	printer	....	in reply	....
		reply	....	in their	....

Additional words				their	
busy	....	Phrases/intersection		require- ments	....
lay	....	in order to	....	well known	....

3A The Modern Art Company

Circular letter about products produced by the paper industry.

Dear Sirs

Our Company has been in the paper industry[10] for the last fifty years, and has always produced paper[20] of very good quality. We would like to expand our[30] business and we plan to distribute our products by the[40] day after receipt of order for distances of up to[50] fifty miles. If headed paper is needed, the delivery date[60] will, of course, depend on printing requirements.

If you are[70] interested in our new service, we shall be very pleased[80] for you to call here at any time to discuss[90] the range of the services we can offer.

Yours faithfully[100]

(The shorthand for this passage is printed on page 76.)

3B The Modern Art Company

Letter of enquiry about the supply and printing of headed paper.

Dear Sir

Thank you for your letter of 16 March.[10] Our Company is very interested in your products, particularly as[20] you can deliver so soon after receipt of order.

I[30] have one or two questions: I would like to ask[40] you whether the cost of your products is lower for[50] large orders; whether your offer of delivery depends on the[60] amount ordered; and whether you can supply headed paper with[70] coloured printing.

As you will see, our Company's colours are[80] blue and gold. Either blue and gold printing on white[90] paper or gold printing on blue paper would be acceptable.[100]

As we deal largely with the art world, you will[110] realise the importance of the quality and character of the[120] materials we use. I wonder whether it would be possible[130] for you to send samples of your work and the[140] type of paper you are able to supply?

Yours faithfully[150]

(The shorthand for this passage is printed on pages 76-7.)

3C The Modern Art Company

Memo asking the Chief Printer to supply samples of printing and paper.

FROM   Sales Department
TO   Chief Printer

Please see the copy[10] letter from The Modern Art Company in reply to our[20] letter of 16 March.

I know that The Modern Art[30] Company is very well known, and I would like to[40] have their custom! Will you please produce samples of the[50] different weights of paper we can supply, both in white[60] and blue. I should also be pleased if you would[70] print samples of their heading in different kinds of layout[80] and type, and colours which you consider would meet their[90] requirements. I should like you to let me have the[100] details as soon as possible so that I can send[110] them before I leave for the summer meeting on 14[120] April. I will also need to have the necessary information[130] in order to reply to the points made in their[140] letter. Have you yourself any observations which you think should[150] be made on this matter?

Many thanks for your help.[160] I do realise that it will make a very considerable[170] amount of work for you at a very busy time.[180]

(The shorthand for this passage is printed on page 77.)

20

CHAPTER 4
Starting a building business

All three letters in this section concern a loan needed to start a new building business. The first is a letter to the bank requesting a loan (100 words); the second is a reply from the bank asking for further details (150 words); and the third (180 words) supplies the required details as to how the loan would be used by the new business.

4A Word list

account		start		grant	
bank		street		John	
brother		such		loan	
build		west		terms	
forward					

Derivatives

possibility

produc-tion

Additional words

applica-tion

live	
look	
office	
side	
small	
some/sum	

Phrase/intersections

building business

I look forward

your Bank

4B Word list

about		much	
above		over	
advant-age		perhaps	
again		property	
along		regard	
capital		short	
example		size	
how		special	
June		talk	
long			
money			
more			

specialist	

Additional words

appoint-ment	
into	
lease	
propose	

Phrase

set out	

Derivatives

enable	

4C Word list

back		house		late	
belief		immedi-ate		mind	
electricity		July		myself	
first		land		pay	
grow					

22

plant		Additional words		for sale	
suggest		available		I believe there is	
water		borrow		in the first place	
within		job			
yard		telephone		in the past	

Derivatives		Phrases		£16,000	16.6
believe		as we have		we have been	
later					
past		at first			

4A Starting a building business

Letter to a bank requesting a loan to start a business.

Dear Sirs

I should like to start a small building[10] business with my brother, John West, who lives next to[20] me at 3 High Street, and I should be grateful[30] if you would consider me for a loan. We have[40] both had an account with your Bank for some considerable[50] time.

My brother and I have worked in the building[60] industry for 10 years, he on the production side and[70] I in the office.

I look forward to hearing from[80] you as to the possibility of my application being granted,[90] and to your terms for such a loan.

Yours faithfully[100]   (*The shorthand for this passage is printed on page 78.*)

4B   Starting a building business

Letter from the bank in reply to the request for a loan.

Dear Sir

I have received your letter of 30 June[10] regarding a possible loan to enable you to start a[20] building business.

I shall need more information before the matter[30] can be considered further. I shall need to know the[40] size of the loan you require, and more details about[50] the proposed business. For example, is the money needed to[60] buy or lease property or is it needed to buy[70] machinery? Is the loan needed for a long or short[80] term, and how much capital will you yourself be able[90] to put into the business?

If you wish to take[100] advantage of our services, perhaps you will let me have[110] the information required, as set out above. I will then[120] write to you again as soon as possible to make[130] an appointment for you to come along to see our[140] Small Business Specialist and talk over the matter.

Yours faithfully[150]

(The shorthand for this passage is printed on page 78-9.)

4C   Starting a building business

Letter to the bank giving details of requirements in respect of the application for a loan.

Dear Sir

Thank you for your letter of 3 July[10] about my application for a loan.

The amount I wish[20] to borrow is £16,000, of which £10,[30]000 is required for the lease of a Yard for[40] the first 2 years, and £6,000 to buy[50] plant and machinery. My brother and I can each put[60] £10,000 into the business as working capital to[70] pay for electricity, water supply, telephone, the cost of insurance[80] and materials for immediate use.

I should like the loan[90] to be for 4 years in the first place, but[100] hope to pay it back within 2 years.

We plan[110] to undertake small building jobs at first, and later, as[120] the business grows, to buy land and build houses for[130] sale. We have been asked to do small building jobs[140] in the past, and I believe there is need in[150] the town for a business such as we have in[160] mind.

I should be grateful for your help and will[170] make myself available at any time you suggest.

Yours faithfully[180]

(The shorthand for this passage is printed on page 79.)

CHAPTER 5
Appointment of a Personal Assistant

This section begins with an advertisement for a Personal
Assistant (100 words), followed by a letter in support of an
application from a Mrs Masters (150 words). The third passage is
a memo from the Personnel Manager to the Head of the
Marketing Department giving details of the arrangements he is
making for the appointment (180 words).

5A   Word list

according	part	latest	
age	people	speech	
drive	personal		
education	provide	**Additional words**	
effect	river	assistant	
experience	road	manager	
general/ generally	run	process	
	speak	salary	
get	than	team	
market			
November	**Derivatives**	**Phrase/intersection**	
operate	effective	later than	

26

marketing
depart-
ment

5B   Word list

act		move		trust-worthy	
ago		now			
become		position		**Additional words**	
carry		regret		appoint	
cause		she		class	
complete		sound		computer	
continue		support		promoted	
December		trust		study	
even				typist	
her		**Derivatives**			
know-ledge		ability		**Phrases/intersection**	
left		action		carried out	
marry		completely		in reply to your letter	
master		comple-tion		with this company	

5C Word list

another		ought		Additional words	
away		principal/ principal-ly/ principle		applicant	
but				attach	
check/ cheque		since		conveni-ent	
degree		subject		post	
far		view		reference	
history					
list		**Derivatives**		**Phrase/intersection**	
morning		interview		so far	
name		notice		your depart-ment	
only		took			

5A Appointment of a Personal Assistant

An advertisement for an experienced Personal Assistant to help in running the Marketing Department.

The Modern Art Company
8 River Road
Blue Town

We[10] need an experienced Personal Assistant to help in the effective[20] running of our Marketing Department. Operating as part of a[30] small team, you should have a good general education, clear[40] speech and be able to get on well with people.[50] Word processing experience would be an advantage.

We operate from[60] up-to-date offices with the latest office machinery.

Salary[70] according to age and experience.

Must be able to drive.[80] Company car provided.

Write for further information to the Personnel[90] Manager. Applications should be received no later than 10 November.[100]

(The shorthand for this passage is printed on page 80.)

5B Appointment of a Personal Assistant

A letter in support of an application for the position of Personal Assistant to the Marketing Manager.

Dear Sir

MRS ANN MASTERS

In reply to your letter[10] of 15 December, I am pleased to support the application[20] of Mrs Ann Masters for the position of Personal Assistant[30] to your Marketing Manager.

Mrs Masters started as a typist[40] with this Company 10 years ago, on completion of her[50] business studies course. She was soon promoted to become Personal[60] Assistant to the Manager of our Sales Department. She showed[70] an interest in her work and was well liked by[80] everyone in the office. She continued her education at evening[90] classes, and now has a sound knowledge of computers. Mrs[100] Masters left the Company last year when she married and[110] moved south.

Her work was always carried out to the[120] best of her ability. She is completely trustworthy, and I[130] am sure that, if you were to appoint her, you[140] would have no cause to regret your action.

Yours faithfully[150]

(The shorthand for this passage is printed on pages 80-81.)

5C Appointment of a Personal Assistant

Memo about arrangements for interviews and regarding Mrs Ann Masters' application.

TO   Head of Marketing Department

FROM   Personnel Manager

Since agreeing[10] a short-list of applicants for the post of Personal[20] Assistant in your Department, I have received another good application,[30] from a Mrs Ann Masters. As you were away, I[40] took up references, but have so far received only one,[50] which I attach for you to see, together with her[60] application. I will let you have the other references as[70] soon as I receive them. As you will see, she[80] has had considerable experience, and is at present studying for[90] a degree with History of Art as her principal subject.[100] Shall I add her name to the short-list?

Would[110] the morning of 20 November be a convenient time for[120] you to hold the interviews? I have checked that the[130] interview room is free at that time. If not, will[140] you please suggest another time and date. We ought to[150] interview before the end of the month in order to[160] leave time for the successful applicant to give a month's[170] notice.

If you agree, I will make the usual arrangements.[180]

(The shorthand for this passage is printed on pages 81-2.)

CHAPTER 6
House for sale

This section concerns the work of a property services company. An advertisement (100 words) offering The Old Farm House for sale starts the section. The second passage is a letter of enquiry about the house and the possible sale of the client's own house (150 words). The third passage is a letter making arrangements for the viewing of The Old Farm House and giving a valuation of the client's own property (180 words).

6A Word list

bed	fully	stone
built	heat	value
coal	home	walk
condition	lead	window
door	minute	yet
east	oil	
except	old	**Derivatives**
face	open	exceptional
family	picture	farmland
farm	play	highly
few	price	ideal
fire	sit	

32

over-
looking

smaller

unusual/
unusually

Additional words

central

centre

fit

kitchen

recom-
mend

Phrase

central
heating

6B Word list

afternoon

could

develop

however

just

keep

king

less

opportun-
ity

reach

reason

recent

sell

wonder-
ful/
wonder-
fully

Derivatives

develop-
ment

reason-
able

recently

replace

sold

unless

valuation

Additional words

Mary

ninety

Phrases

at home

let me
have

recently
been

very
much

which
you have

6C Word list

August ....

friend ....

go ....

instruc-
tion ....

might ....

quick ....

rather ....

result ....

though ....

Tuesday ....

turn ....

yesterday ....

Derivatives

ahead ....

higher ....

owner ....

return ....

Additional words

holiday ....

key ....

reduce ....

sincerely ....

Phrases

as a result ....

let me
know ....

rather
than ....

3 pm ....

yours
sincerely ....

6A House for sale

An advertisement by John Stone Property Services, giving details of The Old Farm House, which is for sale.

John Stone
Property Services

THE OLD FARM HOUSE

An interesting[10] property of exceptional value.

Unusual 3-bedroomed stone-built house[20] in very good condition.

Only a few minutes' walk from[30] the centre of town, yet with well-planned grounds overlooking[40] farmland.

Oil-fired central heating with open coal fire in[50] sitting room, which faces south-east and has two large[60] picture windows.

Fully fitted kitchen, with door leading to playroom.[70]

Large master bedroom and 2 smaller bedrooms.

All the usual[80] offices.

Parking for 3 cars.

An ideal family home.

Viewing[90] highly recommended.

Price £121,000[100]

(*The shorthand for this passage is on pages 82-3.*)

6B House for sale

Letter asking for an appointment to view a house for sale and about arrangements for the sale of another house.

Dear Sir

Thank you for sending me details of the[10] property known as The Old Farm House, which you have[20] for sale. I should very much like to see it[30] and will telephone to arrange a time. However, I can[40] come only during the afternoon.

I could not buy the[50] property unless I sold my present home for a reasonable[60] price. If I do buy The Old Farm House, will[70] you undertake the sale of my house for me? It[80] was built just about ninety years ago and offers a[90] wonderful opportunity for development. All the windows have recently been[100] replaced in keeping with the character of the house.

I[110] should be grateful if you would let me have a[120] valuation of my house. I am at home almost every[130] afternoon, and can be reached in the mornings at the[140] office on 6421.

Yours faithfully

Mary King[150]

(The shorthand for this passage is printed on page 83.)

6C House for sale

Letter to Mrs King to confirm appointment to view.

Dear Mrs King

As a result of seeing your house[10] yesterday, I am now able to give you a valuation[20] of £92,000, though for a quick sale[30] it might be necessary to reduce this figure to about[40] £86,000.

As soon as you let me[50] know whether you wish me to act for you regarding[60] the sale, and whether you wish to accept the lower[70] figure for a quick sale rather than have the house[80] advertised at the higher figure, I will go ahead with[90] the necessary arrangements. Will viewing be possible only in the[100] afternoons, or could the key be left with a friend[110] during the mornings if necessary?

The owners of The Old[120] Farm House have now returned from holiday, and I have[130] made an appointment for you to view the property next[140] Tuesday, 25 August at 3 pm. Will you[150] please let me know if this is not convenient.

I[160] shall look forward to receiving your instructions in the near[170] future as to the sale of your house.

Yours sincerely[180]

(The shorthand for this passage is printed on page 84.)

CHAPTER 7
Motorway garage

This section begins with a memo (100 words) asking for a letter to be delivered to The Motorway Garage. The second passage (150 words) is the letter to be delivered, which asks the garage to find out why the car will not start; while the third passage (180 words) is a message received from the garage explaining that an electrical fault is the cause of the trouble.

7A Word list

certain	tell	**Additional words**
expect	tomorrow	brown
half	trouble	garage
him	want	journey
motor	written	
quite		**Intersection**
really	**Derivative**	tomorrow morning
situation	buyer	

7B Word list

body	connect	down	
brake/ break	doubt	electric	

38

engine	try	hit
find	weak/week	loose
happen	went	mechanic
loss		message
mine	**Derivatives**	repair
miss		
off	accord-ance	**Phrases/intersection**
opinion	agree-ment	at the same time
power	broken	in accord-dance with the
radio	connec-tion	
regular	driver	last time
same	lost	no doubt
several		some attention
simple	**Additional words**	
stop	faulty	

authority	cover	official
burn	danger	quarter
came	earth	ready
case	hand	real

said

six

state

table

therefore

until

wire

found

insurer

officially

Additional words

catch

due

fault

guarantee

Derivatives

electrical

Phrases/intersection

11 am

first thing

on the other hand

this morning

this will

7A Motorway garage

Memo asking for arrangements to be made for a letter to be delivered to The Motorway Garage.

TO   General Office

FROM   Chief Buyer

Will you please ask[10] John to deliver the attached letter to The Motorway Garage[20] when he goes to the bank tomorrow morning? I know[30] it will add half a mile to his journey, but[40] I do want to be certain that they have written[50] instructions. Tell him it is quite important, as I really[60] need another car on Wednesday, and thank him for his[70] trouble. If the garage telephones tomorrow while I am out,[80] please put the call through to Mary Brown – she knows[90] the situation and will be expecting the call. Many thanks.[100]

(The shorthand for this passage is printed on pages 84-5.)

7B Motorway garage

A letter to the garage asking them to correct an electrical fault in a company car.

Dear Sirs

My Company car has broken down. It is[10] my opinion that the electrics are faulty, as the car[20] lost power and the radio went off. This has happened[30] several times recently, but the last time the engine stopped[40] completely. Could your mechanic come to the office to try[50] to find the trouble? No doubt it could be something[60] quite simple like a loose connection. If not, perhaps you[70] would have the car in for a check and do[80] the regular service at the same time. The bodywork also[90] needs some attention as another car hit the driver's door[100] when parking last week. Could you also repair the door[110] for me?

In accordance with the agreement, will you please[120] make another car available for my use while mine is[130] off the road? If you telephone while I am out,[140] Miss Brown will take a message for me.

Yours faithfully[150]

(The shorthand for this passage is printed on pages 85-6.)

7C Motorway garage

Message received from the garage about the repair of the car.

Message from Mary Brown to Chief Buyer

The Motorway Garage[10] came for your car this morning at 11 am[20] and telephoned this afternoon at 2 pm. They said[30] that the trouble with the car is caused by an[40] electrical fault where the covering of an earth wire had[50] been burnt away, and that in its present state there[60] is a real danger that the car might catch fire.[70] It will take six days to replace the wiring, and[80] it will be done under guarantee. On the other hand,[90] the work on the body of the car will not[100] be covered by guarantee. They will, therefore, not start on[110] this work until they receive your authority.

The garage will[120] provide you with a car while yours is being repaired,[130] and this will be ready first thing tomorrow.

I have[140] found the insurance papers and left them on your table[150] in case you want to write to the insurers officially[160] about the repair to the body of the car. We[170] paid the amount due for this quarter only last week![180]

(The shorthand for this passage is printed on page 86.)

CHAPTER 8
Activity holidays

This section consists of three letters. The first (100 words) is in reply to an enquiry about activities available on the holidays advertised; the second (150 words) is to book a holiday with horse riding for one of the children in the family, and the third (180 words) confirms the booking and gives details of the riding lessons and competitive events.

8A Word list

air/heir	heart	easy
beautiful	horse	national
bread/bred	love	none
cheap	milk	scenery
children	nation	or
English	October	speciality
fish	school	**Additional words**
fly	second	bake
follow	seen/scene	choose
food	**Derivatives**	hotel
full	activity	include
health	beauty	ride

44

8B Word list

baby

begin

boy/buoy

child

happy

limit

mean

Saturday

September

spend/
spent

third

us

young

Derivatives

apart

certainly

Additional words

accom-
modate

double

Jones

ridden

share

single

son

suitable

wife

Phrases

if possible

in the
meantime

some time
ago

very far

8C Word list

across

animal

care

comfort

commit

competi-
tion

control

employ

event

field

final

foot

Friday

himself

improve	....	competi-tive	....	lesson	....
measure	....			path	....
pleasure	....	herself	....	progress	....
serious	....	improve-ment	....		
whole/hole	....	instructor	....		

Phrases

I am pleased	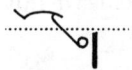
takes part	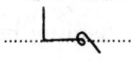
to be able to	

Additional words

accommo-dation	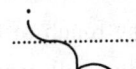
confirm	....

Derivatives

comfort-able	

46

8A Activity holidays

Letter describing holiday activities, such as fly fishing and horse riding, and accommodation in the beautiful scenery of the English countryside.

Dear Mr Love

Thank you for your letter. We offer[10] the following open-air activities – fly fishing, horse riding, sailing[20] and walking, from March to October.

Our farm hotel, set[30] in beautiful scenery in the heart of the English countryside,[40] is within easy reach of the motorway. Our food is[50] second to none, and includes milk from our farm and[60] home-baked bread.

Children are welcome and we offer cheap[70] weekend breaks outside school holidays. Health and beauty weeks are[80] our speciality and you can choose either full or half[90] board.

We are highly recommended in national papers.

Yours sincerely[100]

(The shorthand for this passage is printed on page 87.)

8B Activity holidays

Letter to Mrs Jones booking a holiday and asking about horse riding instruction.

Dear Mrs Jones

Thank you for sending me details of[10] your activity holidays. My wife and I would like to[20] book a week's holiday beginning the third Saturday in September,[30] if you can accommodate us. We have a very young[40] baby, who would share our room, and a boy aged[50] 10, so we would need one single and one double[60] room. If possible, we would like rooms next to each[70] other, or certainly not very far apart.

Will you please[80] let me know whether the horse riding you offer is[90] suitable for a child of my son's age. He has[100] ridden a few times on a friend's horse, but this[110] was some time ago. His experience is limited and he[120] has had no real instruction.

I hope to hear from[130] you soon. In the meantime we look forward to spending[140] a very happy holiday with you.

Yours sincerely

John Love[150]

(The shorthand for this passage is printed on pages 87-8.)

48

Letter confirming the holiday booking for Mr Love.

Dear Mr Love

In reply to your letter received today,[10] I am pleased to be able to offer you a[20] double room, with a single room nearby, for a week[30] beginning Saturday, 20 September.

Your son is the ideal age[40] to begin serious horse riding lessons. Our instructor, who has[50] been employed by us for the past 7 years, is[60] very committed to his work and is always in full[70] control of the situation. The one-hour lessons are followed[80] by rides across fields and along footpaths away from roads.[90] During the final lesson of the week, on the Friday,[100] each child takes part in competitive events, when his or[110] her progress is measured and improvement noted. Each child rides[120] the same horse the whole week, and is responsible for[130] caring for the animal himself or herself.

All our accommodation[140] is first class, and I am sure you will be[150] very comfortable with us. I look forward to the pleasure[160] of meeting you and your family, and should be grateful[170] if you would confirm your booking in writing.

Yours sincerely[180]

(The shorthand for this passage is printed on pages 88-9.)

CHAPTER 9
Work experience

Three letters comprise this section. The first is to ask a firm if
they will accept two students on work experience (100 words),
the second (150 words) gives details of the students involved, and
the third (180 words) is from the firm as a result of the students'
work experience, reporting on their interests and suitability for
the kind of work they undertook.

9A Word list

difficulty .... respect .... widely ....

equal .... say ....

fact .... strange .... **Additional words**

February .... thought .... prepare ....

learn .... wide .... students ....

memory .... without ....

north .... **Phrases**

organisa- .... **Derivatives** from their ....
tion

profit .... equally .... in fact ....

50

beyond		worth	
dress			
engineer		**Derivative**	
express			
		useful	
indeed			
science		**Additional words**	
teach			
Thursday		appropri-ately	
what		classroom	
whatever		contribu-tion	
whenever		extend	

main
practice/practise
request
Phrases/intersection
as his
Engineer-ing Dep-artment
of course
will be
worth while

common		exist		moment
credit		girl		neither
demand		imposs-ible		nor
differ		language		perfect
discover		method		plain
exchange				sense

ship 

system 

those 

upon 

Derivatives

perfectly 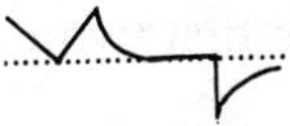

shipment 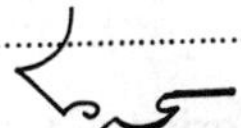

younger 

Additional words

college 

enjoy 

export 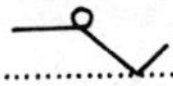

file 

keen 

staff 

suitability 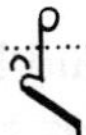

vacancy 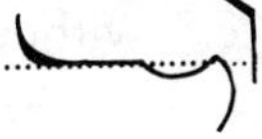

Phrases

common sense 

I am able to 

it is impossible 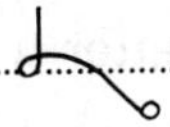

should be pleased 

side of the 

they were 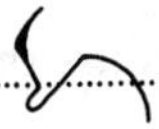

to take part 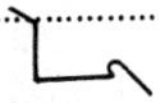

9A Work experience

A letter to Mrs North requesting placements for students on work experience.

Dear Mrs North

I wonder whether you would be prepared[10] again to employ two of our students on work experience,[20] without pay, for the first two weeks of February?

Last[30] year's students learned widely from their experience with your organisation[40] and returned with happy memories, knowing that the business world[50] was not the strange place they had thought. I should[60] like this year's students to profit equally, and should be[70] grateful if you could help in this respect. I realise[80] that this may present difficulties, and will understand if you[90] say you cannot, in fact, help this year.

Yours sincerely[100]

(The shorthand for this passage is printed on page 89.)

9B Work experience

A letter giving details of students John Day and Ann King going on work experience.

Dear Mrs North

Thank you for your letter. I am[10] very pleased indeed that you are able to have 2[20] students on work experience, and will send them to see[30] you on Thursday at 11 am, as requested.

The[40] job you have in mind for John Day in your[50] Engineering Department will be ideal, as his main interest is[60] science. Ann King is on a business studies course.

Experience[70] of this kind is very worth while, and I would[80] like to express my thanks to you for making it[90] possible. It enables the students to put into practice what[100] we teach them and to extend their experience beyond the[110] classroom.

The students will, of course, be expected to arrive[120] on time, dress appropriately, and do whatever is required of[130] them whenever asked. I hope that they will make some[140] useful contribution towards the work of your office.

Yours sincerely[150]

(The shorthand for this passage is printed on pages 89-90.)

54

9C Work experience

A letter from Mrs North to Mr West, reporting on the work experience of the two students.

Dear Mr West

Now that Ann and John have completed[10] their two weeks with us, I am able to send[20] my report. Both fitted perfectly into our organisation and were[30] equal to demands made upon them.

Ann showed a great[40] deal of common sense for a girl of her age.[50] John was keen to discover how our computer system worked,[60] and how our files differed from those in College. Ann[70] was interested in the export side of the business and[80] the shipment of goods, as she feels that this is[90] where she could use her second language. They were both[100] a credit to the College.

Neither Ann nor John presented[110] difficulty. They were interested in our methods of work, and[120] it was plain that our younger staff enjoyed exchanging views[130] with them. I would not doubt for a moment their[140] suitability for a job here, but it is impossible to[150] say if a vacancy will exist when they have completed[160] their course.

We should be pleased to take part again[170] should you wish to place students with us.

Yours sincerely[180]

(The shorthand for this passage is printed on pages 90-91.)

CHAPTER 10
Safety – accident in the office

This section consists of three memos. The first (100 words) is to the Safety Officer, to try to find the cause of an accident to a child visiting the firm: the second (150 words) is the Safety Officer's reply, stating that it was probably due to a trailing wire; and the third (180 words) is a memo from the Safety Officer to employees, drawing their attention to the need to be aware of any faults which might cause accidents.

10A Word list

attempt	why	**Additional words**
cry	wrong	accident
cut		claim
deep	**Derivatives**	floor
fall	deeply	reception
father	did	reception-ist
gentlemen	fell	unfortun-ately
mother	heard	visit
purpose	officer	**Phrases**
record	safety	at the time
safe	saw	did not

56

10B Word list

appear		rule		Additional words	
arm		save		aid	
behind		sign		articles	
brought		step		caught	
drink		sweet		coin	
frequent		tried		drop	
gave		warm		hospital	
hard				memo	
heavy		**Derivatives**			
inform		employee		**Phrases/intersections**	
news		frequently		I will	
night		heavily		arrange	
once		kept		insurance form	
pence		probably		it appears	
probable		ran		once again	
rest					
round					

10C Word list

announce

bad

balance

base

because

front

light

little

nature

never

nothing

object

poor

pull

read

remember

straight

wise

Derivatives

announce-
ment

clearly

immedi-
ately

natural

remind

Additional words

lift

listen

switch

technician

trailing

Phrases

at once

do not

10A Safety – accident in the office

Memo asking the Company's Safety Officer to attempt to find the cause of an accident.

FROM Manager

TO   Safety Officer

As you may know, a[10] child, visiting the office with her mother and father, fell[20] in the reception area and cut her head deeply. The[30] receptionist was recording the purpose of the visit at the[40] time, and did not see what happened. She heard the[50] child cry and then saw her on the floor. There[60] were two gentlemen present, but unfortunately they did not see[70] what happened either. Will you please attempt to find out[80] what went wrong and why, and take any necessary action.[90] It is quite possible there could be an insurance claim.[100]

(The shorthand for this passage is printed on page 91.)

10B Safety – accident in the office

Memo from the Safety Officer explaining the cause of the accident and the steps taken as a result.

FROM Safety Officer

TO   Manager

ACCIDENT IN RECEPTION AREA

It[10] appears that the child dropped a 10 pence coin and[20] ran after it. She probably caught her foot on a[30] loose wire behind the small, round table. She fell heavily[40] as she tried to save herself, hitting her arm and[50] head on the hard step. The receptionist gave her first[60] aid and a warm, sweet drink. She was taken to[70] hospital and kept overnight for rest and observation.

I have[80] completed and signed the insurance form and sent it off.[90] I have prepared a memo, to be sent to employees[100] to inform them once again of the rules about safety[110] at work. I am of the opinion that the matter[120] of safety is one which must be brought to the[130] notice of employees frequently, maybe in the monthly newsletter. If[140] you agree, I will arrange for articles to be prepared.[150]

(The shorthand for this passage is printed on page 92.)

10C Safety – accident in the office

Memo to employees outlining safety precautions.

TO   All employees

FROM   Safety Officer

May I remind you[10] of the need to think of safety at all times.[20] There must, for example, be no trailing wires from machines.[30] Never leave electrical machinery switched on overnight as this could[40] cause a fire. Check the machines you use for signs[50] of any bad connection and report any faults immediately to[60] the technician.

A light must always be left on where[70] the natural lighting is poor. Nothing should be left in[80] front of fire doors.

Do not stand on anything without[90] a firm base and, where possible, pull rather than lift[100] large objects. Do not carry too many heavy things at[110] once because they might over-balance. It is little use[120] being wise after the event!

Please inform me if, in[130] your opinion, there are any other areas of danger that[140] we have not noticed, and make sure that you read[150] all fire notices and listen to any announcements regarding safety.[160]

Remember that all accidents must always be reported and recorded[170] straight away, with the cause of the accident clearly stated.[180]

(*The shorthand for this passage is printed on page 93.*)

CHAPTER 11
Complaint by customer

This section consists of three letters: the first (100 words) is a letter of complaint about a faulty dress; the second (150 words) is in reply to the complaint; and the third (180 words) expresses dissatisfaction with the way the complaint has been handled.

11A   Word list

big		Sunday		shop	
bought		surprise		twice	
city		waist/ waste		wash	
dye/die				wore	
enough		**Derivatives**			
longer		undone		**Phrases**	
red		unsatis- factory		no longer	
satisfac- tory				this was not	
seam/ seem		**Additional words**		two weeks ago	
sometimes		refund			
store					

62

11B Word list

bring	Derivatives	Phrases
desire	manufac-turer	I am sorry
manufac-ture	owing	it is not
mass	sewn	it would have been
often		this matter
owe	Additional words	very well
sort	assure	we assure you
still	complaint	we trust that you will
test	dry	
	sorry	
	unfortun-ate	

11C Word list

altogether	life	Derivatives
between	strong	consider-ably
force	true	does
itself	woman	satisfac-torily
least	women	

Additional words		faded		wear	

aim

attractive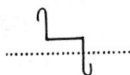

settle

television

Phrase

at least

11A Complaint by a customer

A letter returning a faulty dress to a store.

Dear Sir

I bought the enclosed red dress from your[10] city store two weeks ago. I wore it twice and[20] then washed it, ready for a family party last Sunday.[30] To my surprise I found that, not only had part[40] of a seam come undone, but the waist was no[50] longer big enough and the dye had run.

While I[60] realise that sometimes a faulty article can get into the[70] shops, this was not a cheap dress. This is most[80] unsatisfactory, and I should be grateful if you would refund[90] the money I spent. The receipt is enclosed.

Yours faithfully[100]

(The shorthand for this passage is printed on page 94.)

11B Complaint by a customer

Letter to Mrs Black in reply to her complaint.

Dear Mrs Black

I am sorry to hear of your[10] unfortunate experience with one of our dresses. However, I have[20] had the seam sewn again and the waist let out[30] to the right size. Our dresses are of a high[40] quality, not mass-produced, and they sell very well. All[50] our goods have to pass a manufacturer's test, so I[60] was very surprised to receive your complaint.

You stated that[70] you washed the dress, but it would have been better[80] if it had been dry-cleaned. I suggest that you[90] do this in future. It is not often we receive[100] a complaint of this sort, owing to the care we[110] take with our products, and we trust that you will[120] still be happy to shop here.

Thank you for bringing[130] this matter to our notice. We assure you of our[140] desire to be of service at all times.

Yours sincerely[150]

(The shorthand for this passage is printed on pages 94-5.)

11C   Complaint by a customer

Letter to Mr White from Mrs Black expressing dissatisfaction about the way her complaint has been dealt with.

Dear Mr White

Further to my complaint, I have received[10] your letter, together with my dress. I find the whole[20] business most unsatisfactory. Your firm is well known, with advertisements,[30] aimed at women, on television and in national papers. The[40] modern woman does not expect to pay so much money[50] for a dress with such a short life. If the[60] dress needed dry-cleaning, then it should have carried instructions[70] to this effect.

I still cannot wear the dress; the[80] colour has faded considerably and this shows where it has[90] been let out at the front of the waist.

The[100] dress itself is attractive, the fault being in the manufacture.[110] It is true that you have repaired the dress, but[120] it is altogether unsatisfactory, and I feel that I have[130] a strong case at least for the exchange of my[140] dress for a new one or for a refund. I[150] am sending the dress back to you. I trust we[160] can settle this matter satisfactorily between us and that I[170] shall not be forced to take further action.

Yours sincerely[180]

(The shorthand for this passage is printed on page 95.)

66

CHAPTER 12
Official opening of building

The first passage (100 words) is a letter asking a representative of the Government to perform the official opening of the extension made to their building by a computer company. The second passage (150 words) is a memo asking the Publicity Manager to research facts which can be used in the Opening speech, and the third (180 words) is part of the speech made at the official opening.

12A Word list

cold

direct

government

iron

January

million

Monday

rate

steal/steel

weather

Derivative

directors

Additional words

extension

perform

provisionally

Phrases

iron and steel

rate of

12B Word list

	Derivatives		
increase		visitor	
judge	customer	wait	
law	publicity		
ourselves		**Phrases**	
page	**Additional words**	as much as possible	
paint	police		
public	pro- gramme	have been	
tax	research	number of	
told		sort of	

12C Word list

among	relate	whom	
answer	story	whose	
ever	them- selves	yes	
fear	touch		
govern	truth	**Derivatives**	
labour	voice	employ- ment	
peace/ piece	war	growth	
political	watch	happiness	

remove		Additional words		Phrases/intersection	
shortage		declare		Ladies and Gentlemen	
truly		expansion			
unem-ployment		ladies		with you	
				your Company	

12A Official opening of building

A letter asking a representative of the Government to perform the official opening of the extension to a computer firm's building on the site of an old iron and steel works.

Dear Mr Hope

My firm has manufactured iron and steel,[10] and now computers, for the past 85 years on[20] this site. We have a £6 million extension, due[30] to be completed in January, if the present rate of[40] progress is not held up by the very cold weather.[50] My Directors would be most grateful if you, as the[60] representative of the Government responsible for Trade and Industry, would[70] perform the official opening for us, provisionally planned for Monday,[80] 7 May.

I look forward to hearing from you and[90] hope that you will be able to accept.

Yours sincerely[100]

(The shorthand for this passage is printed on page 96.)

12B Official opening of building

Memo asking the Publicity Manager to supply the Government representative with facts for his speech, and to inform police of the event.

FROM   General Manager

TO   Publicity Manager

OFFICIAL OPENING OF EXTENSION[10]

Mr Hope has agreed to open our extension on 7[20] May. Will you please carry out some research for material[30] on which he can base his speech. Send as much[40] as possible and he can judge for himself what to[50] use to paint the sort of picture he wishes to[60] present. Say that increased profits enabled the Company to pay[70] the recent higher tax without passing this on to customers.[80] Before sending off this information, wait until the programmes have[90] been printed, enclose a copy, and draw his attention to[100] the information on page 2, which he might find useful.[110]

The Safety Officer has told me that, in the interests[120] of law and order, we ourselves must inform the police[130] of the date and time of the official opening and[140] the number of visitors expected. Will you please do this?[150]

(The shorthand for this passage is printed on pages 96-7.)

12C Official opening of building

Part of the speech made on the occasion of the official opening of the building extension.

Ladies and Gentlemen

I am pleased to be here with[10] you today. I do not wish to make a political[20] speech, but I must touch upon the importance of the[30] computer industry to the nation, and voice the opinion that[40] this will continue to increase, thereby serving the needs of[50] the public. Those among you whose working life has been[60] spent in this industry will have watched its development, governed[70] by and related to the rate of growth of many[80] other industries.

In reply to the question of whether the[90] industry is important both in time of peace and in[100] war, I can answer, with truth, a firm 'Yes'. The [110] expansion of your Company provides employment for many local people –[120] in fact there has now become a shortage of labour[130] in the area, removing, perhaps for ever, the fear of[140] unemployment.

It gives me great pleasure to say to your[150] Company, 'May your success story continue', to wish the employees[160] themselves, on whom so much depends, happiness in their new[170] buildings, and to declare the extension well and truly open.[180]

(The shorthand for this passage is printed on pages 97-8.)

Shorthand key to passages

1A

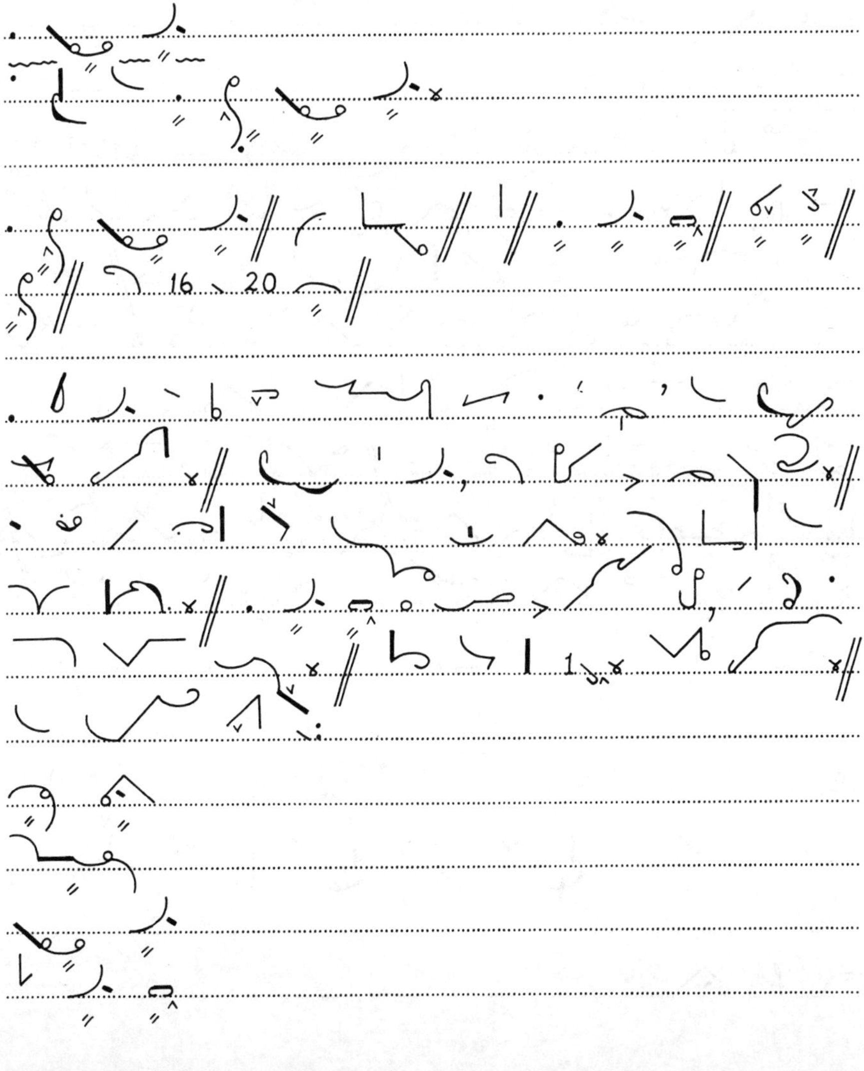

72

16 20

2A

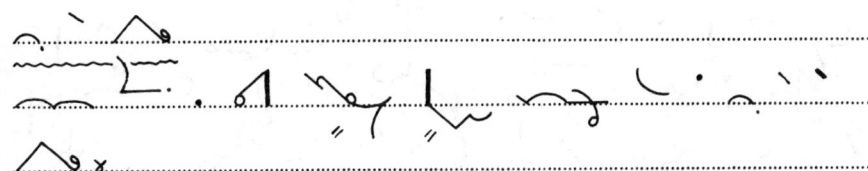

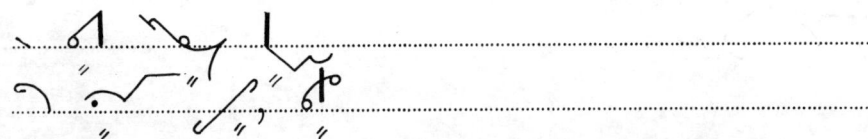

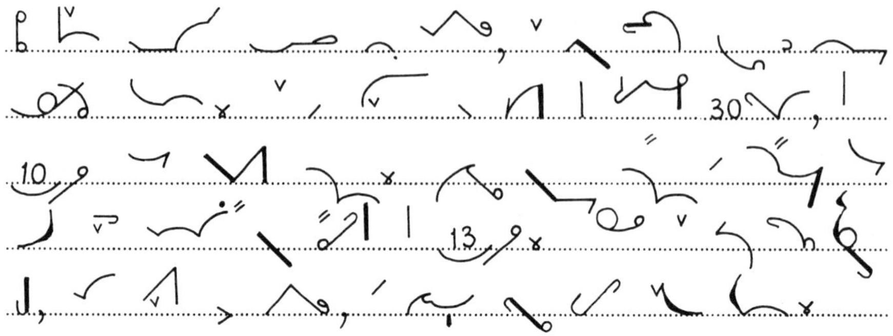

2B

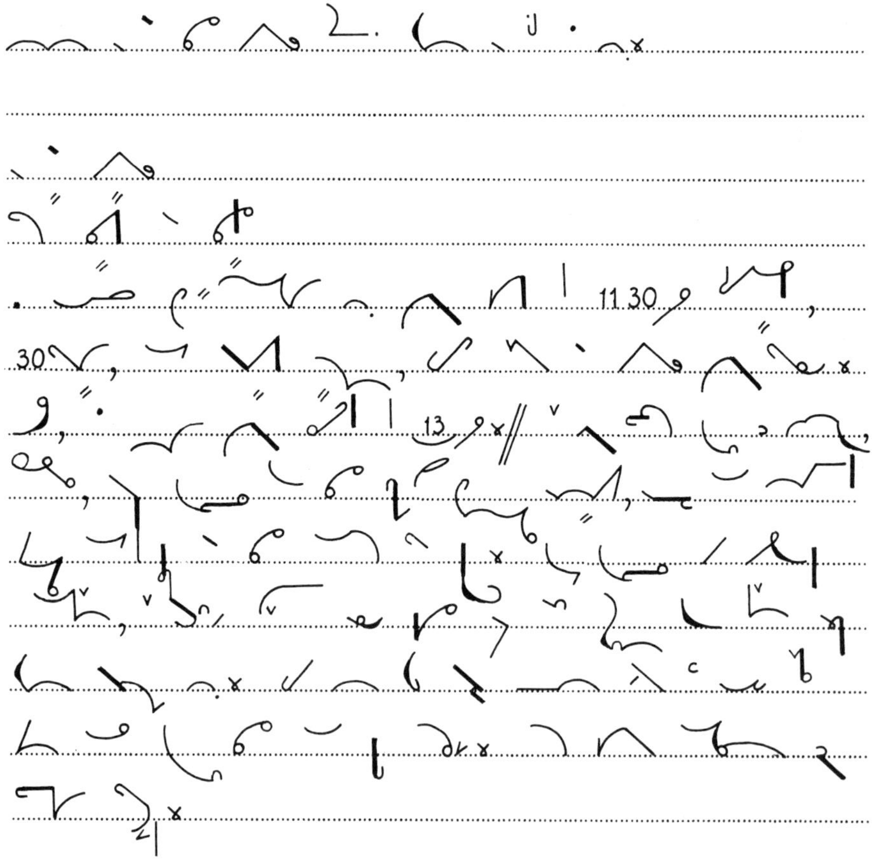

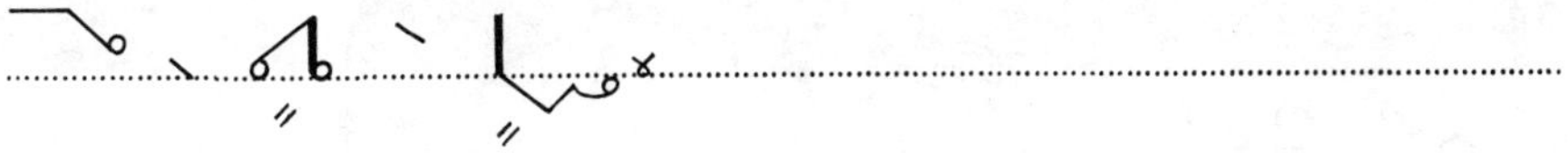

2C

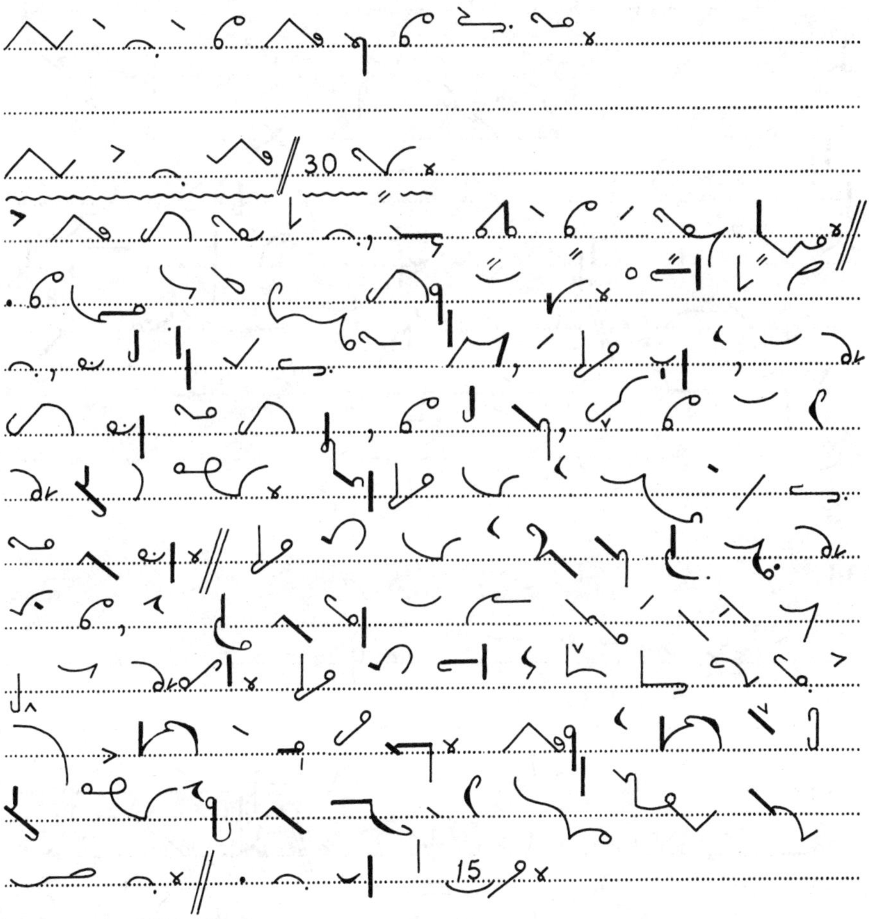

3A

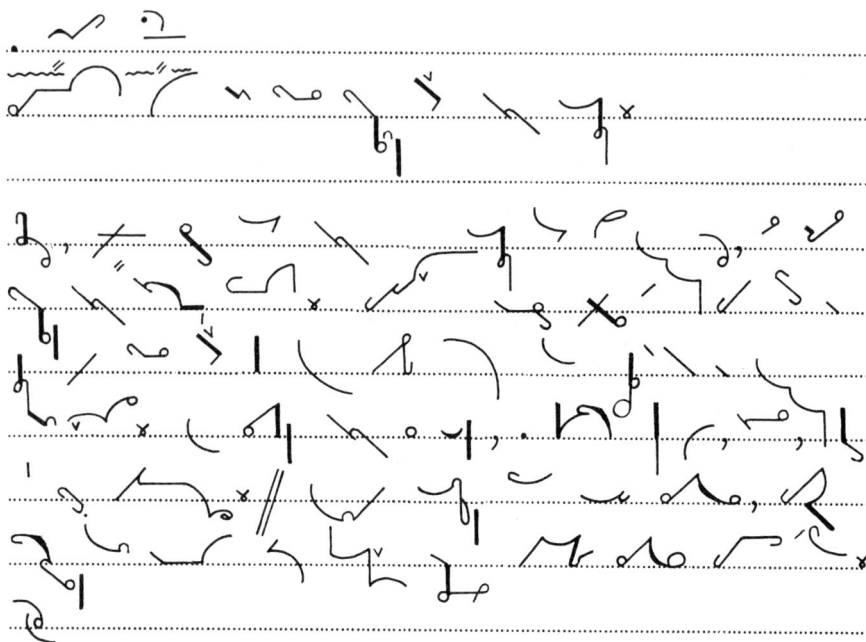

3B

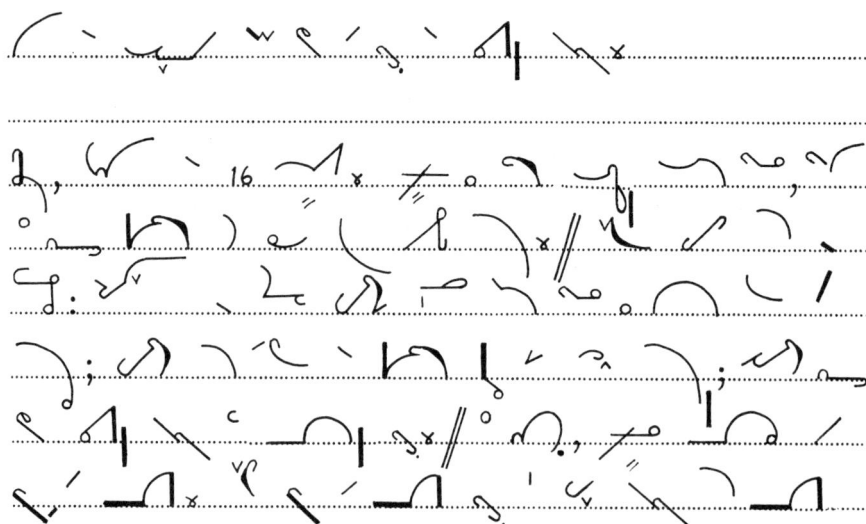

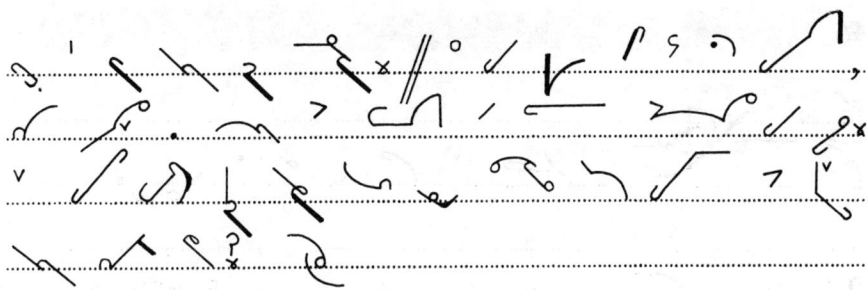

3C

4A

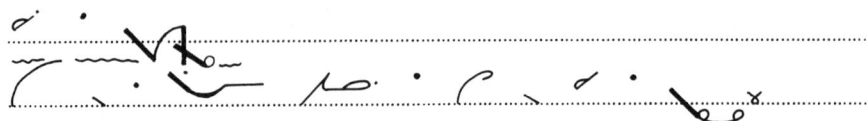

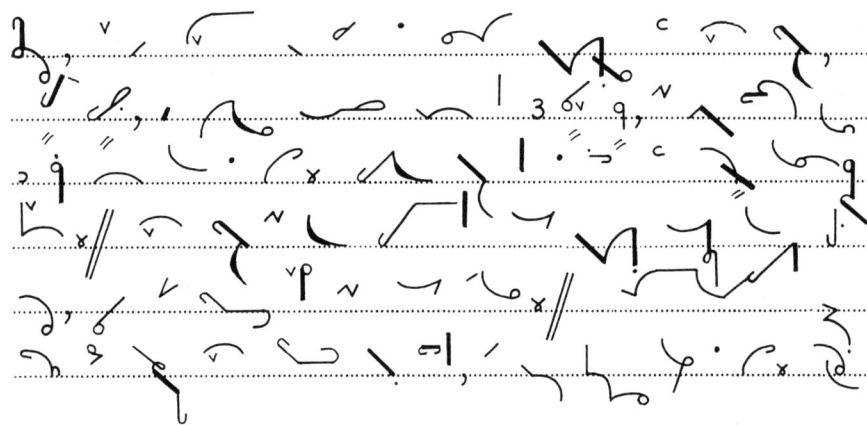

4B

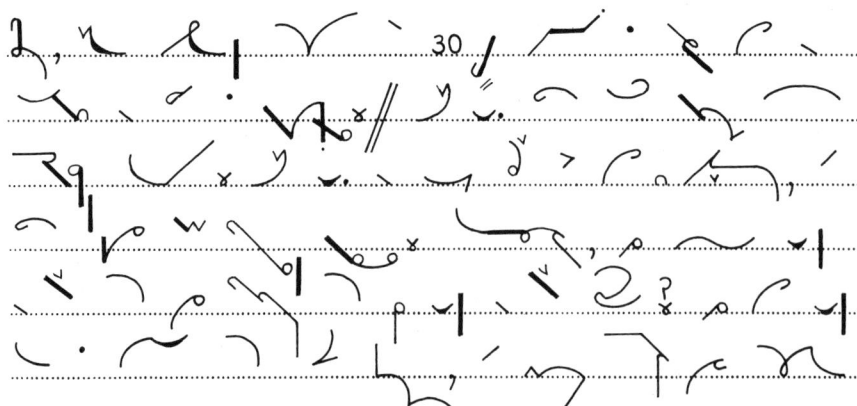

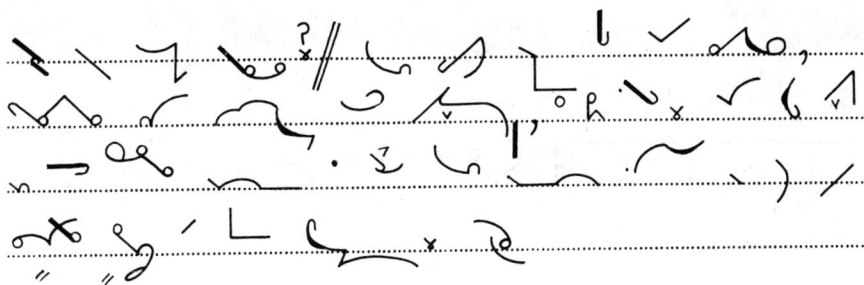

4C

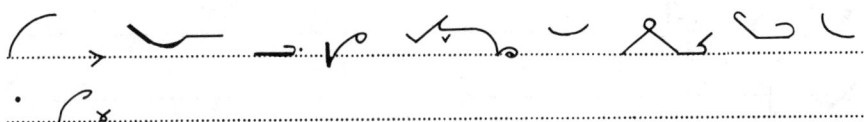

5A

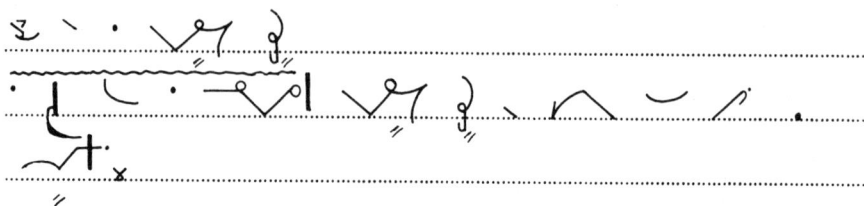

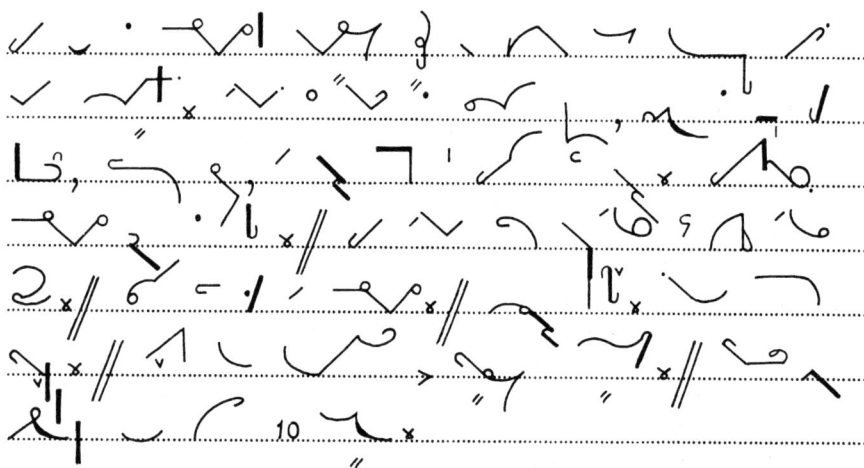

5B

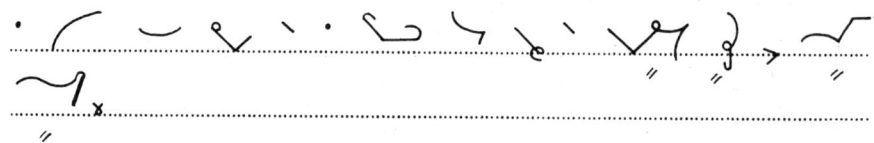

5C

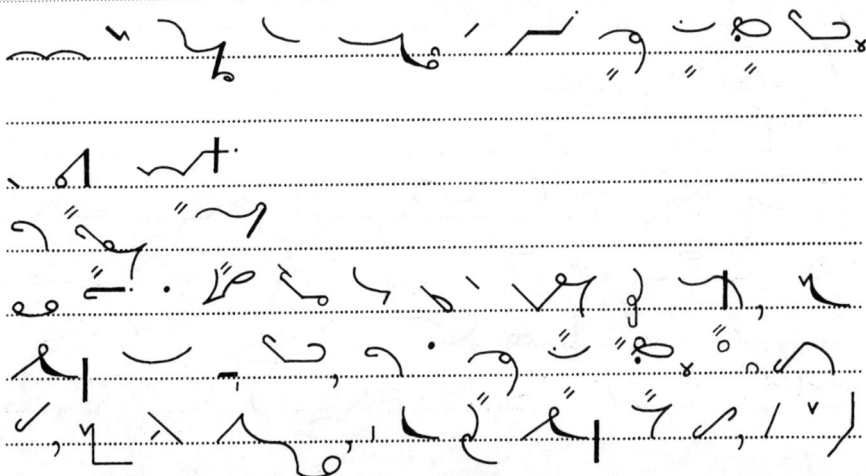

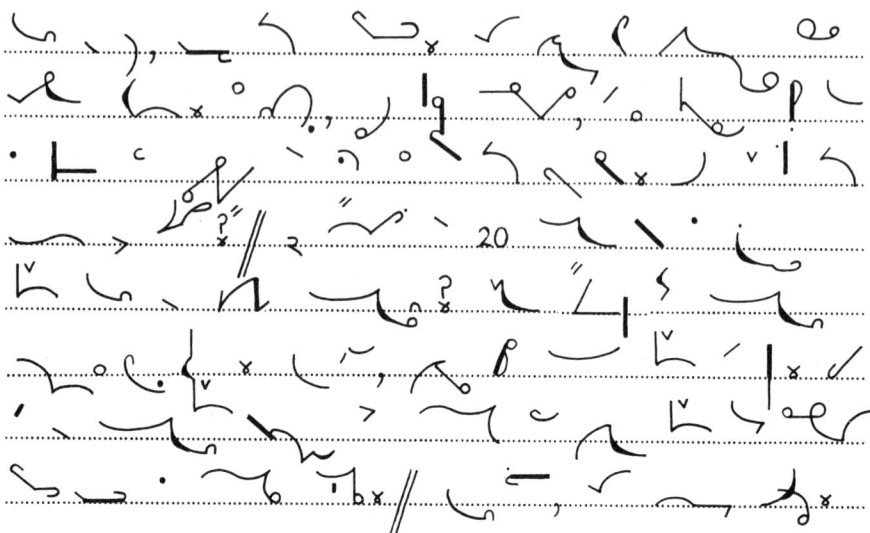

6A

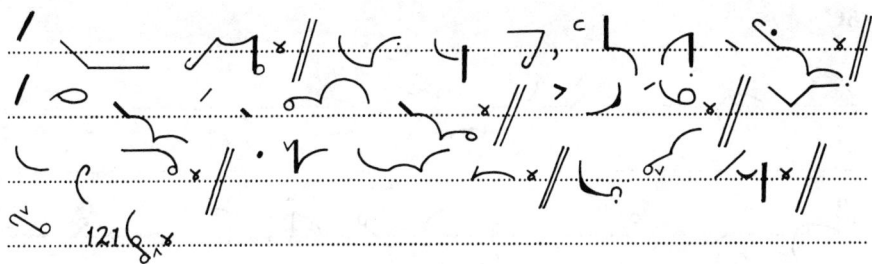

6B

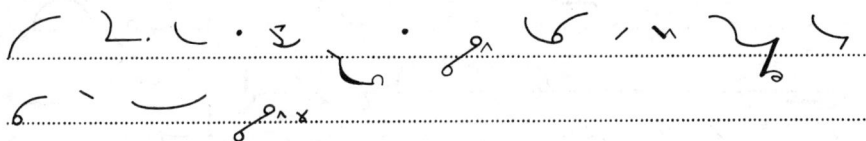

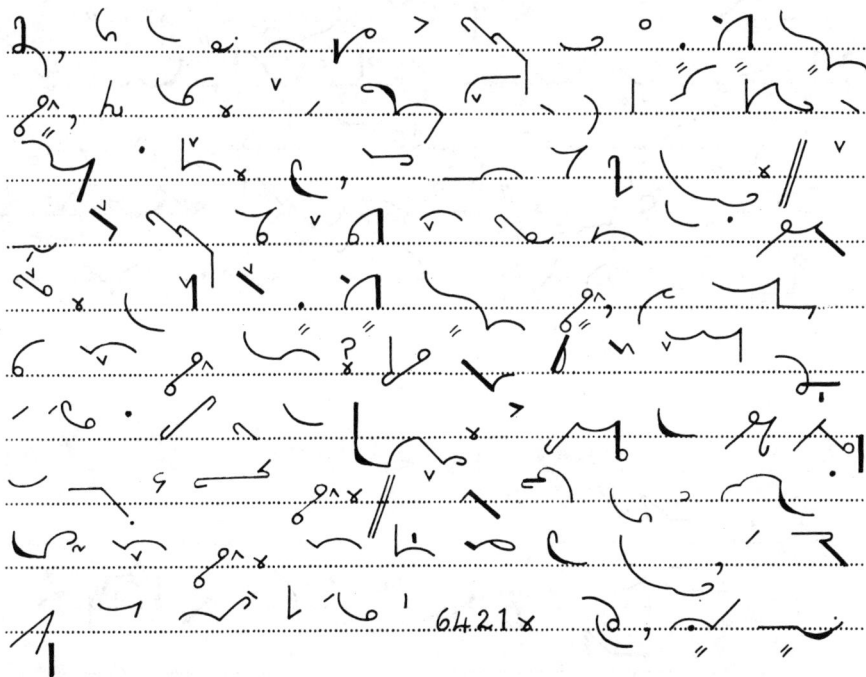

6C

7A

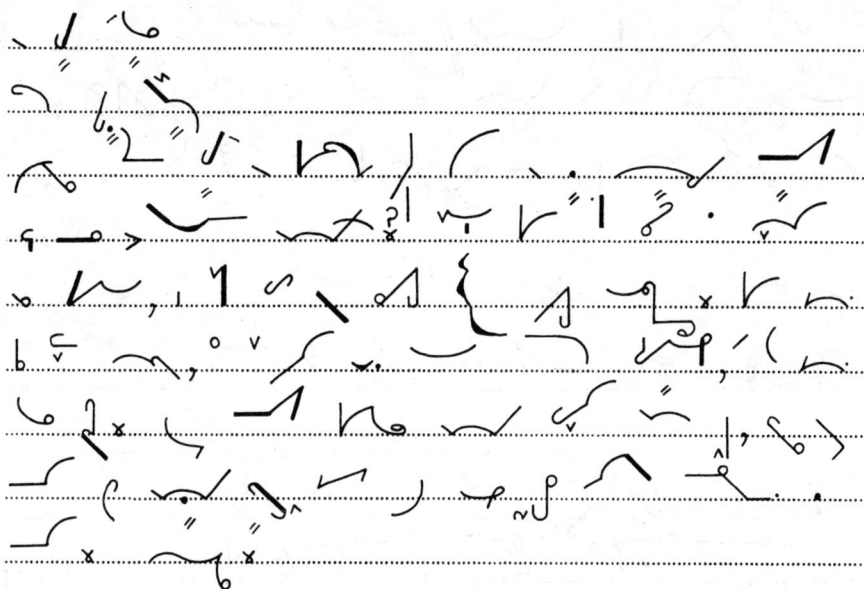

7B

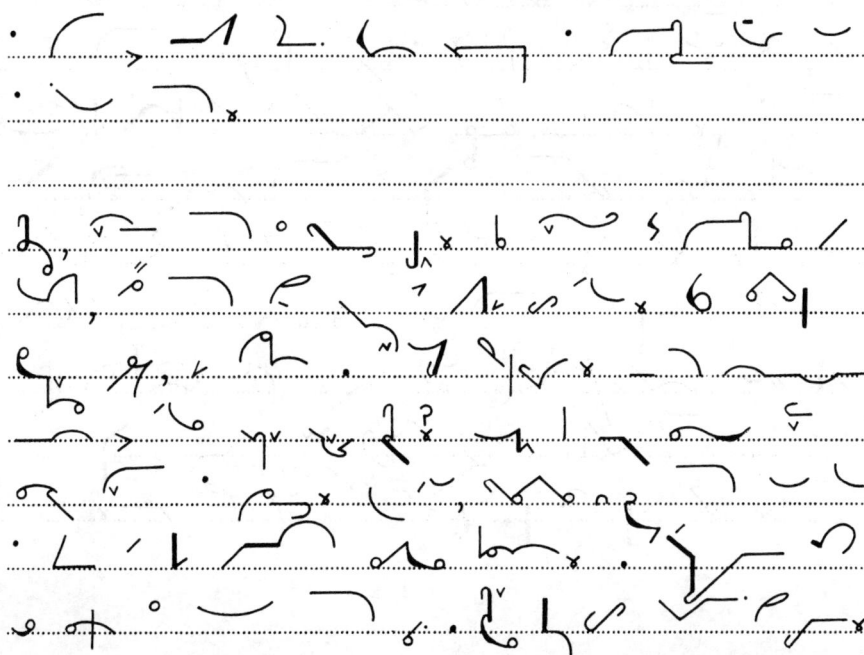

86

7C

8A

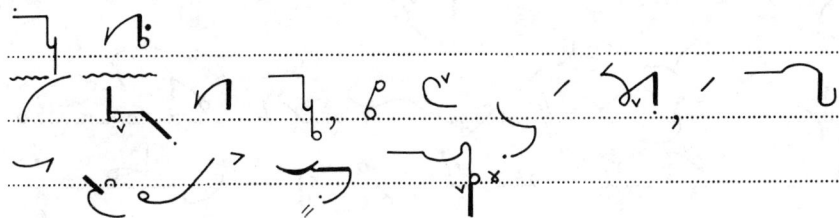

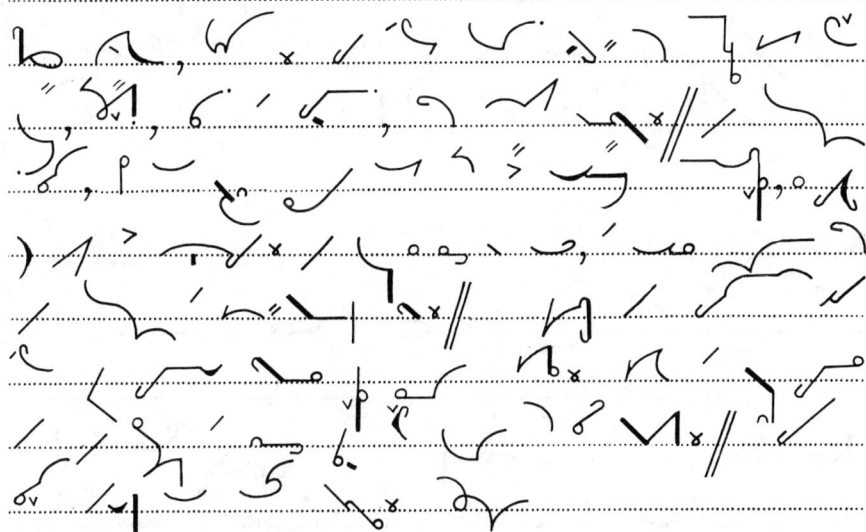

8B

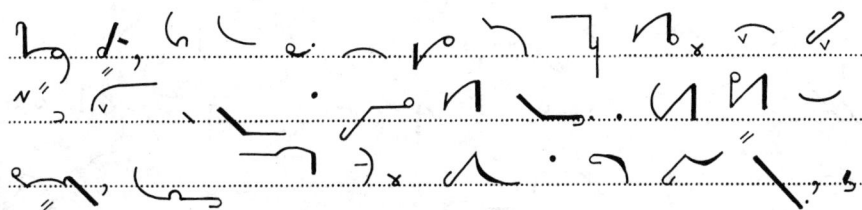

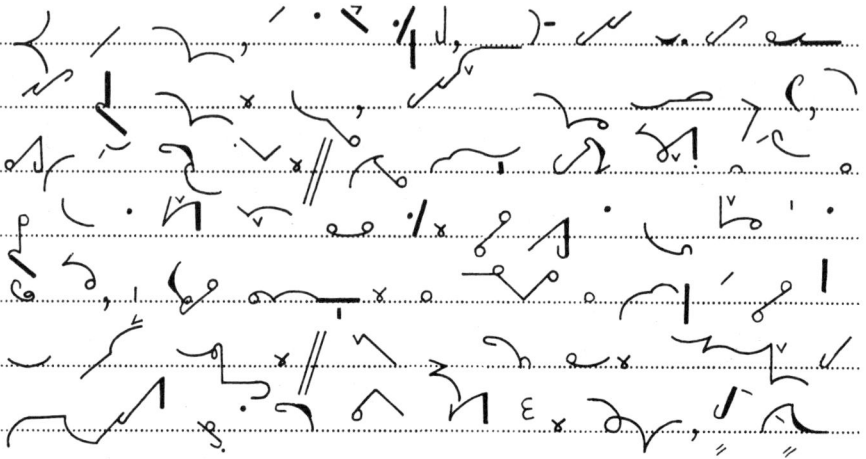

8C

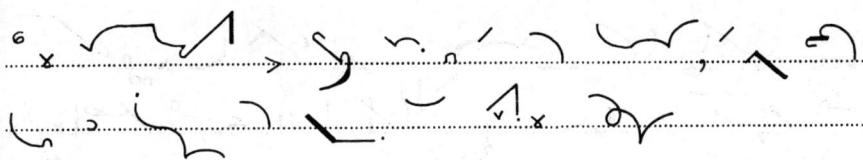

89

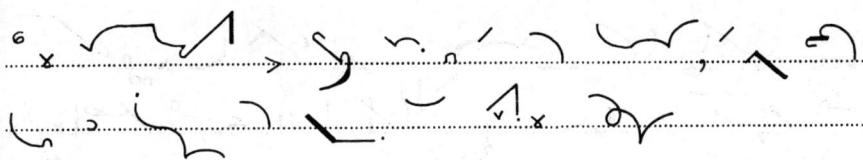

9A

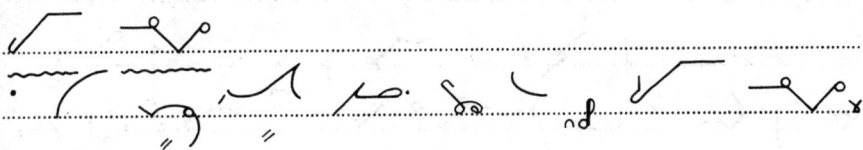

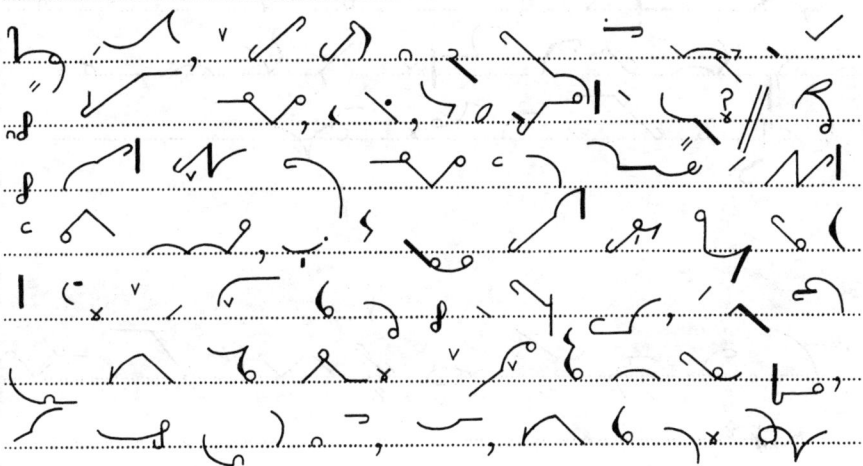

9B

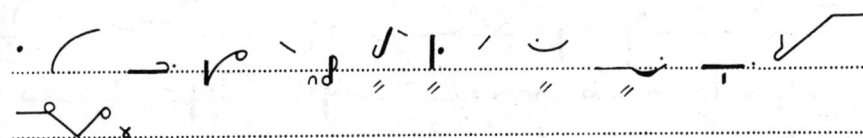

9C

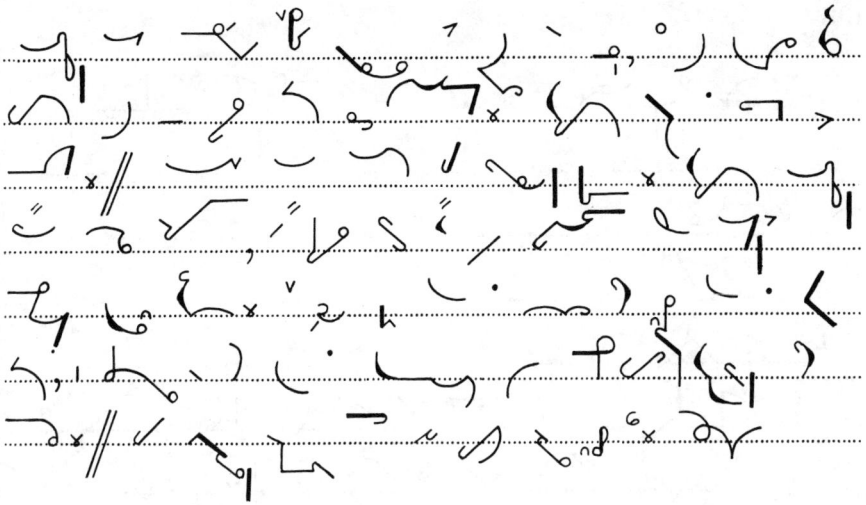

10A

10B

10C

11A

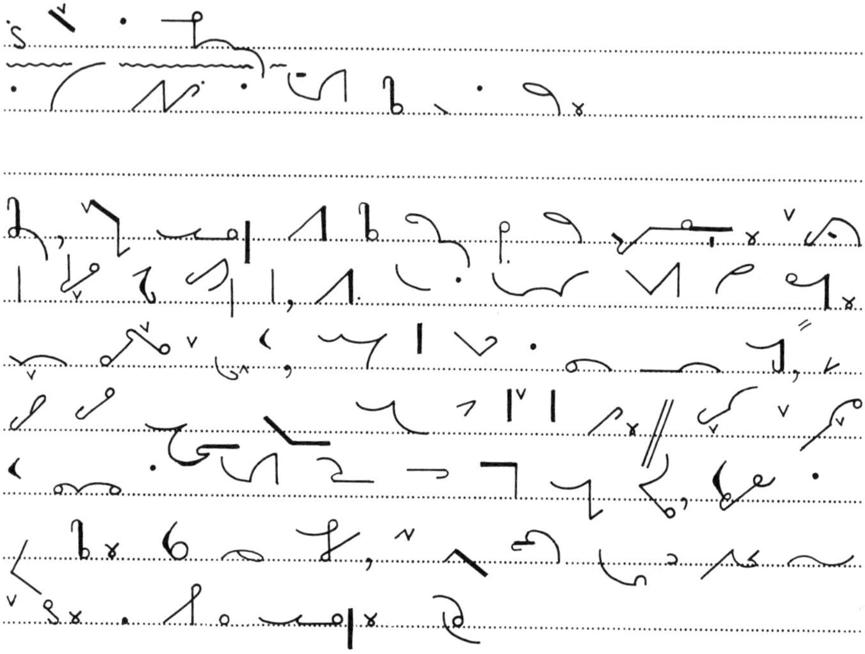

11B

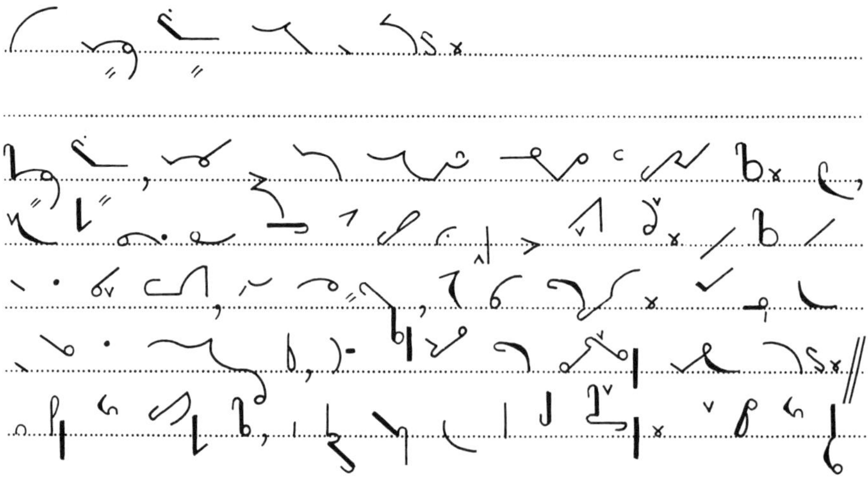

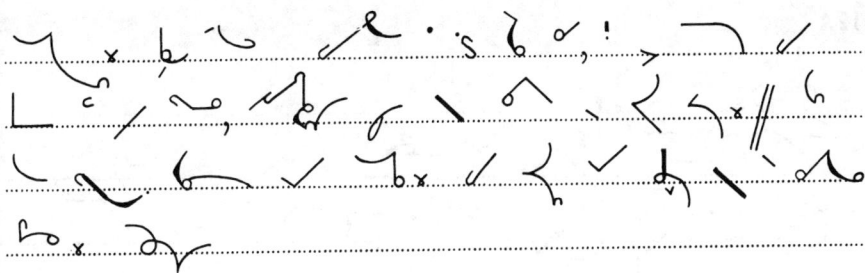

11C

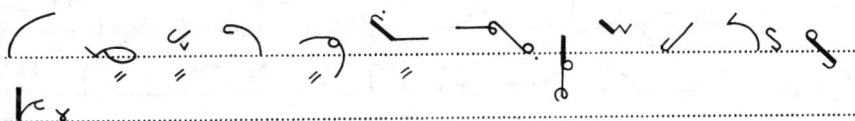

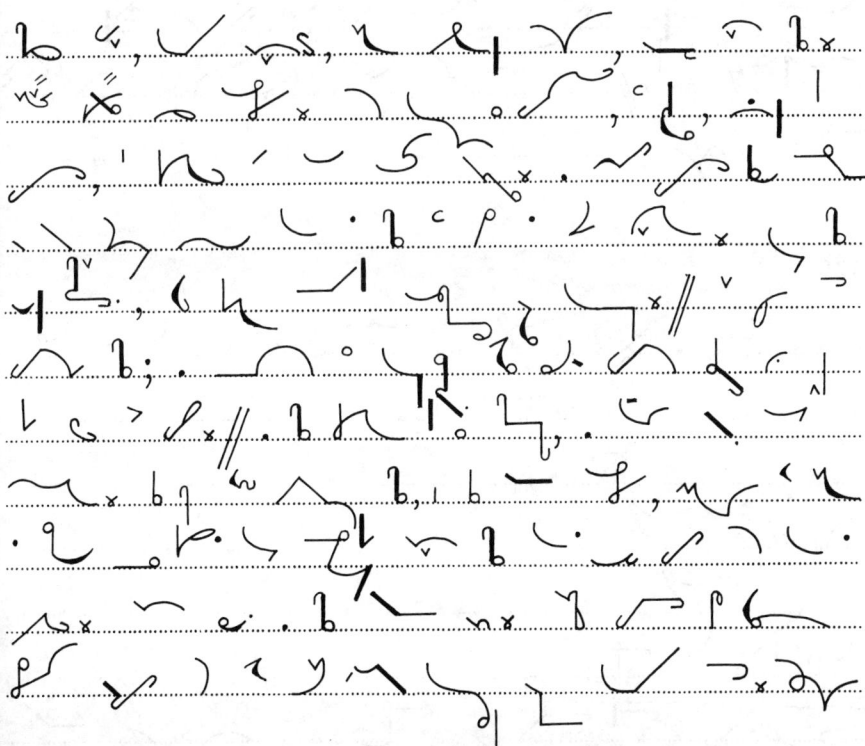

96

12A

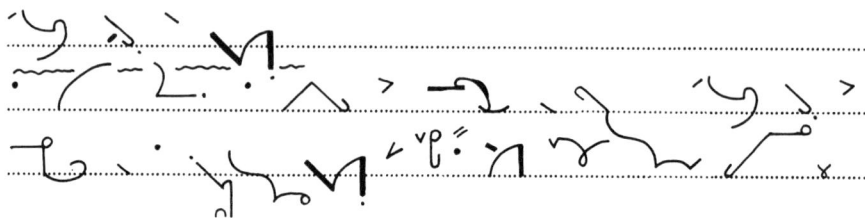

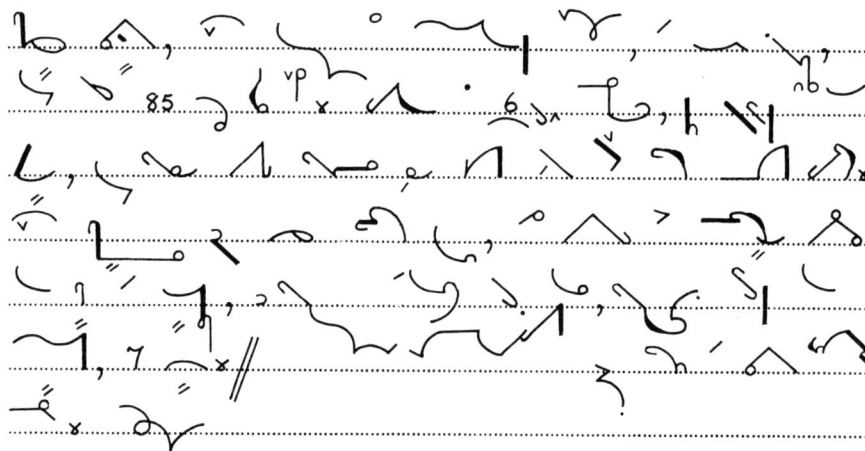

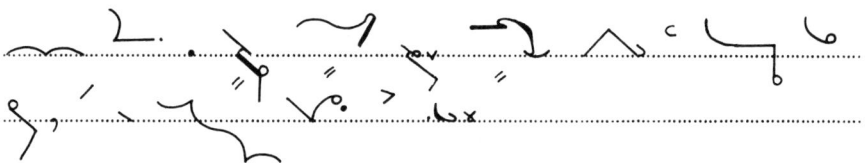

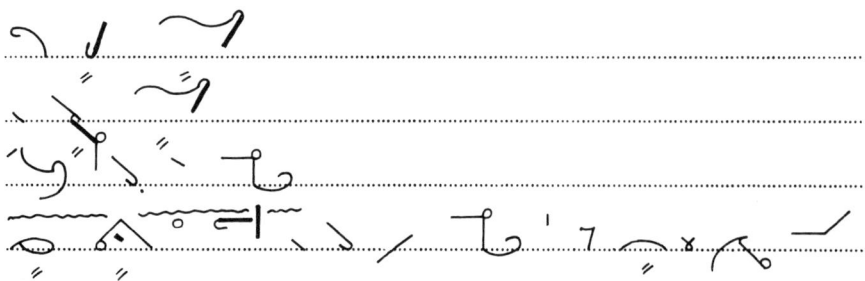

12B

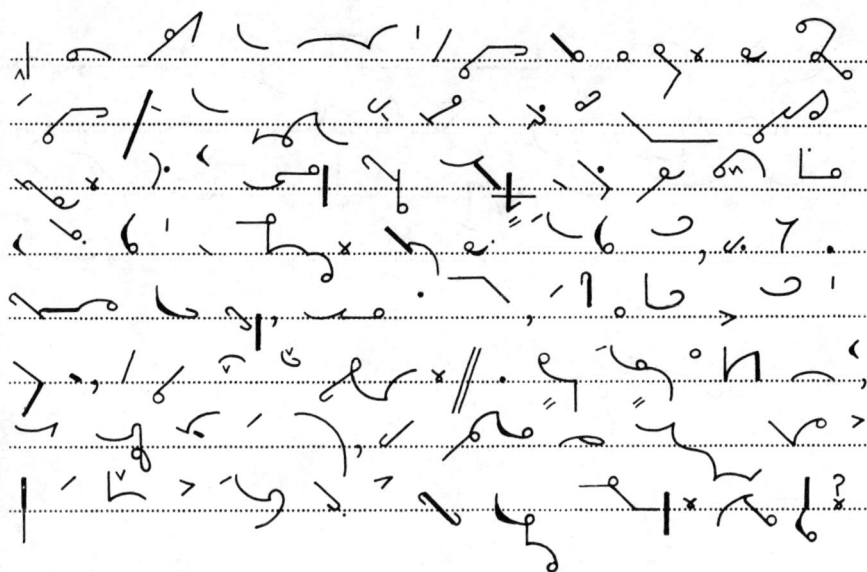

12C

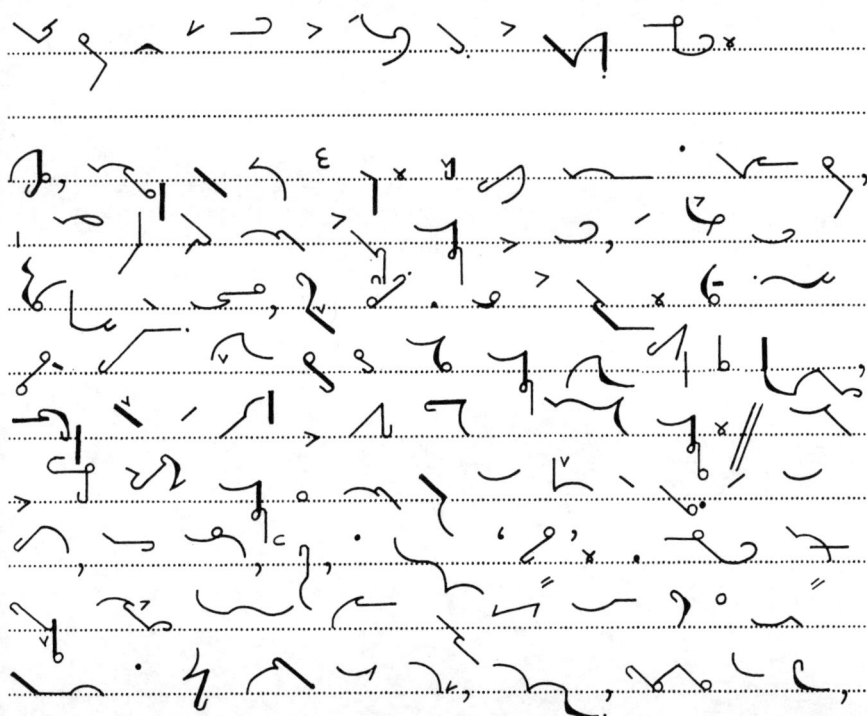

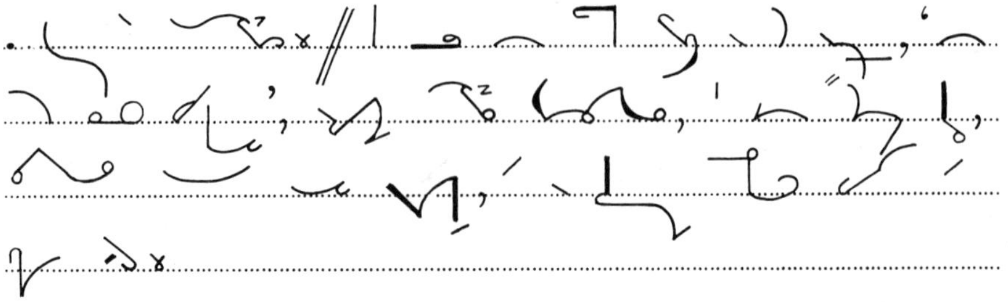

List of 700 Common Words

These outlines represent approximately 68 per cent of the words contained in ordinary English matter*.

a		age		another			
able		ago		answer			
about		agree		any			
above		air		appear			
according		all		April			
account		along		are			
across		also		arm			
act		altogether		art			
add		am		as			
advantage		among		ask			
advertise advertise- ment		amount		at			
after		an		attempt			
afternoon		and		attention			
again		animal		August			
		announce		authority			

* Together with their derivative outlines, these words represent approximately 80 per cent of the words in ordinary English matter.

away		beyond		business	
		big		but	
baby		black		buy	
back		blue		by	
bad		board		bye	
balance		body		call	
bank		book		came	
base		both		can	
be		bought		capital	
beautiful		boy		car	
because		brake		care	
become		bread		carry	
bed		break		case	
before		bring		cause	
begin		brother		cell	
behind		brought		certain	
belief		build		change	
believe		building		character	
best		built		charge	
better		buoy		cheap	
between		burn		check	
				cheque	

chief		control		depend	
child		copy		desire	
children		cost		detail	
city		could		develop	
clean		country		die	
clear		course		differ	
coal		cover		difference difference	
coarse		credit		difficult	
cold		cry		difficulty	
colour		custom		direct	
come		cut		discover	
comfort				distance	
commit		danger		distribute	
common		date		division	
company		day		do	
competition		dear		door	
complete		December		doubt	
condition		deep		down	
connect		degree		dress	
consider		deliver		drink	
continue		demand		drive	

during	event	February
dye	ever	feel
	every	few
each	example	field
early	except	figure
earth	exchange	final
ease	exist	find
east	expect	fire
education	experience	first
effect	expert	fish
either	express	fly
electric	eye	follow
electricity		food
employ	face	foot
end	fact	for
engine	fall	force
engineer	family	form
English	far	forward
enough	farm	free
equal	father	frequent
even	fear	Friday

friend	grow	high
from		him
front	had	himself
full	half	his
fully	hand	history
further	happen	hold
future	happy	hole
	hard	home
gave	has	hope
general generally	have	horse
	he	hour
gentlemen	head	house
get	health	how
girl	hear	however
give	heart	hundred
go	heat	
gold	heavy	I
good	heir	idea
govern	help	if
government	her	immediate
great	here	important importance
ground		

104

impossible		June	left	
improve		just	less	
in			let	
increase		keep	letter	
indeed		kind	life	
industry		king	light	
influence		knew	like	
inform		know	limit	
inform-ation		knowledge	line	
			list	
instruction		labour	little	
insurance		land	live	
interest		language	long	
iron		large	longer	
is		last	look	
issue		late	loss	
it		law	love	
itself		lead	low	
		learn		
January		least	machine	
judge		leave	made	
July			maid	

make		must	
man		my	
manufac-ture		myself	
many			
March		name	
mark		nation	
market		nature	
marry		near	
mass		necessary	
master		need	
matter		neither	
may		never	
me		new	
meal		news	
mean		next	
measure		night	
meat		no	
meet		nor	
memory		north	
method		not	
might		note	
mile			
milk			
million			
mind			
mine			
minute			
Miss			
modern			
moment			
Monday			
money			
month			
more			
morning			
most			
mother			
motor			
move			
Mr			
Mrs			
much			

nothing		open		paper	
November		operate		part	
now		opinion		particular	
number		opport- unity		party	
object		or		pass	
observa- tion		order		pay	
October		organise		peace	
of		organisa- tion		pence	
off		other		people	
offer		ought		perfect	
office		our		perhaps	
official		ourselves		person	
often		out		personal	
oh!		over		picture	
oil		owe		piece	
old		own		place	
on				plain	
once				plan	
one		page		plane	
only		paint		plant	
				play	

please	purpose	record
pleasure	put	red
point		regard
political	quality	regret
poor	quarter	regular
position	question	relate
possible	quick	remember
pound	quite	report
power		represent
present	radio	
price	rail	require
principal principally principle	rate	respect
	rather	responsible -ibility
probable	reach	
product	read	
profit	ready	rest
property	real	result
provide	really	
public	reason	right
publish	receive	river
pull	recent	road

room	seen	simple
round	self	since
rule	sell	sir
run	send	sit
	sense	situation
safe	sent	six
said	September	size
sail	serious	small
sale	serve	so
same	service	some
satisfac-tory	set	sometimes
Saturday	several	soon
save	sew	sort
say	shall	sound
scene	she	south
school	ship	sow
science	short	speak
sea	should	special
second	show	spend
see	side	spent
seem	sign	stand

start	supply	then
state	support	there
station	sure	therefore
steal	surprise	these
steel	sweet	they
step	system	thing
still		think
stone		third
stop	table	this
store	take	those
story	talk	though
straight	tax	thought
strange	teach	thousand
street	tell	through
strong	test	
subject	than	Thursday
success	thank	
such	that	time
suggest	the	
sum	their	together
summer	them	told
Sunday	themselves	tomorrow

too		use		Wednesday	
touch		usual		week	
toward		usually		weigh	
town				well	
trade		value		went	
train		very		were	
tried		view		west	
trouble		voice		what	
true				whatever	
trust		waist		when	
truth		walk		whenever	
try		want		where	
Tuesday		war		whether	
turn		warm		which	
two		was		while	
		waste		white	
under		watch		who	
until		water		whole	
up		way		whom	
upon		we		whose	
us		weak		why	
		weather			

wide		wonderful		wrong	
will		wonder-fully			
window		word		yard	
winter		work		year	
wire		world		yes	
wise		worth		yesterday	
wish		would		yet	
with		wrest		you	
within		write		young	
without		writing		your	
woman		written			
women					

List of derivatives

ability		certainly	did
accordance		clearly	directors
action		comfortable	distribution
activity		competitive	does
agreement		completely	done
ahead		completion	driver
always		connection	easier
announcement		considerable	easy
apart		considerably	effective
		consideration	electrical
beauty			employee
been			employment
believe		customer	enable
broken			equally
buyer		deeply	exceptional
		delivery	
cannot		development	farmland

fell		improvement	natural
felt			none
found		instructor	notice
frequently		insurer	
		interview	officer
given		kept	officially
grateful		known	organiser
greatly			overlooking
growth		largely	owing
		largest	owner
happiness		later	
heard		latest	particularly
heavily		lost	past
held		lower	perfectly
herself			personnel
higher		machinery	possibility
highly		manufacturer	probably
holder		materials	produce
		monthly	production
ideal			publicity
immediately		national	ran

reasonable		sewn		trust-worthy	
receipt		shipment			
recently		shortage		undone	
remind		smaller		unemploy-ment	
remove		sold			
replace		specialist		unless	
represent-atives		speciality		unsatis-factory	
require-ment		speech		unusual/ly	
		stationery		useful	
return		successful			
				valuation	
safety		taken			
satisfactor-ily		took		welcome	
saw		truly		widely	
scenery				younger	
or					

List of additional words

accept

acceptable

accident

accommo-
date

accommo-
dation

admission

aid

aim

applicant

application

appoint

appoint-
ment

appreciate

appropri-
ately

area

arrange

arrange-
ment

arrive

article

assistant

assure

attach

attractive

available

bake

borrow

brown

busy

catch

caught

central

centre

choose

claim

class

classroom

coin

college

complaint

computer

concern

confirm

contribu-
tion

convenient

deal

declare

department

116

discuss	firm	keen
double	fit	key
draw	floor	kitchen
drop		
dry	garage	ladies
due	*or*	lay
	grant	lease
enclose	guarantee	lesson
enjoy		lift
expand	hit	listen
expansion	holiday	loan
export	hospital	local
extend	hotel	loose
extension		
	include	madam
	into	main
faded		manager
faithfully	job	Mary
fault	John	mechanic
faulty	Jones	memo
fifty	journey	message
file		

117

ninety		receptionist		son	
		recommend		sorry	
park		reduce		staff	
path		reference		study	
perform		refund		student	
police		repair		suitable	
post		reply		suitability	
practice/se		request		switch	
prepare		research			
print		ride		team	
printer		ridden		technician	
process				telephone	
programme		salary		television	
progress		sample		ten	
promoted		scent		term	
propose		settle		ticket	
provisionally		share		trailing	
		shop		transport	
range		sincerely		twenty	
realise		single		twice	
reception		site/sight		type	

typist	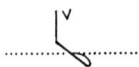	vacancy		wash	
		visit		wear	
unfortun-ate		visitor	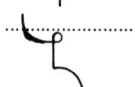	wore	
				wife	
unfortun-ately		wait		wonder	

List of phrases and intersections

able to		carried out	
advertising department		central heating	
as a result		common sense	
as his		Dear Sir or Madam	
as much as possible		did not	
as soon as possible		do not	
as soon as we can		11 am	
as we have		engineering department	
at all times		first thing	
at first		for sale	
at home		from their	
at least		further information	
at once		had not been	
at the same time		has been	
at the time		have been	
best wishes		I am able to	
building business		I am pleased	

I am sorry		in their	
I believe there is	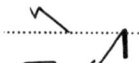	in this matter	
I hope		insurance form	
I look forward		iron and steel	
I will arrange		it appears	
I would like		it is impossible	
if possible	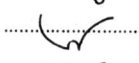	it is not	
if you will		it will be	
in accordance with the	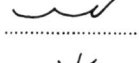	it would be	
in any way		it would have been	
in charge of	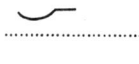	last time	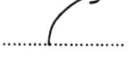
in fact		later than	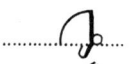
in order to		Ladies and Gentlemen	
in our		let me have	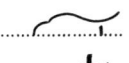
in reply		let me know	
in reply to your letter		marketing department	
in the business		necessary arrangements	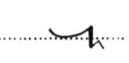
in the country		no doubt	
in the first place		no longer	
in the meantime		number of	
in the past		of course	

on the other hand		they are	
once again		they were	
our Company		this matter	
range of the		this morning	
rate of		this was not	
rather than		this will	
recently been		three months	
sales department		3 pm	
set out		to be able to	
should be pleased		to consider	
side of the		to take part	
£16,000		tomorrow morning	
so far		two thousand	
some attention		two weeks ago	
some time ago		up-to-date	
sort of		very far	
take place		very much	
takes part		very well	
thank you		we assure you	
thank you for your letter		we have been	
their requirements		we shall be	

we trust that you will		worth while	
we would like	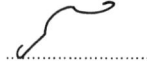	your bank	
well known		your company	
which you have		your department	
will be		your own	
will you please		yours faithfully	
with this company		yours sincerely	
with you			